This Book
Belongs to:

Thank you!

Thank you for buying " Letter Tracing Book for Preschoolers Ages 3-5" book!

If you have any suggestions on how to improve it, or what we can change or add to make it more useful particularly to you, please do hesitate to contact us at activitybook8@gmail.com

We would be more than happy to consider how to apply your suggestion to the next edition.

Without your voice, we can't exist.

Please, support us and leave a review!

We welcome your positive feedback and hope that others will benefit from your expenence.

Start at the dot. Trace the dotted line.
Use the arrow as a guide

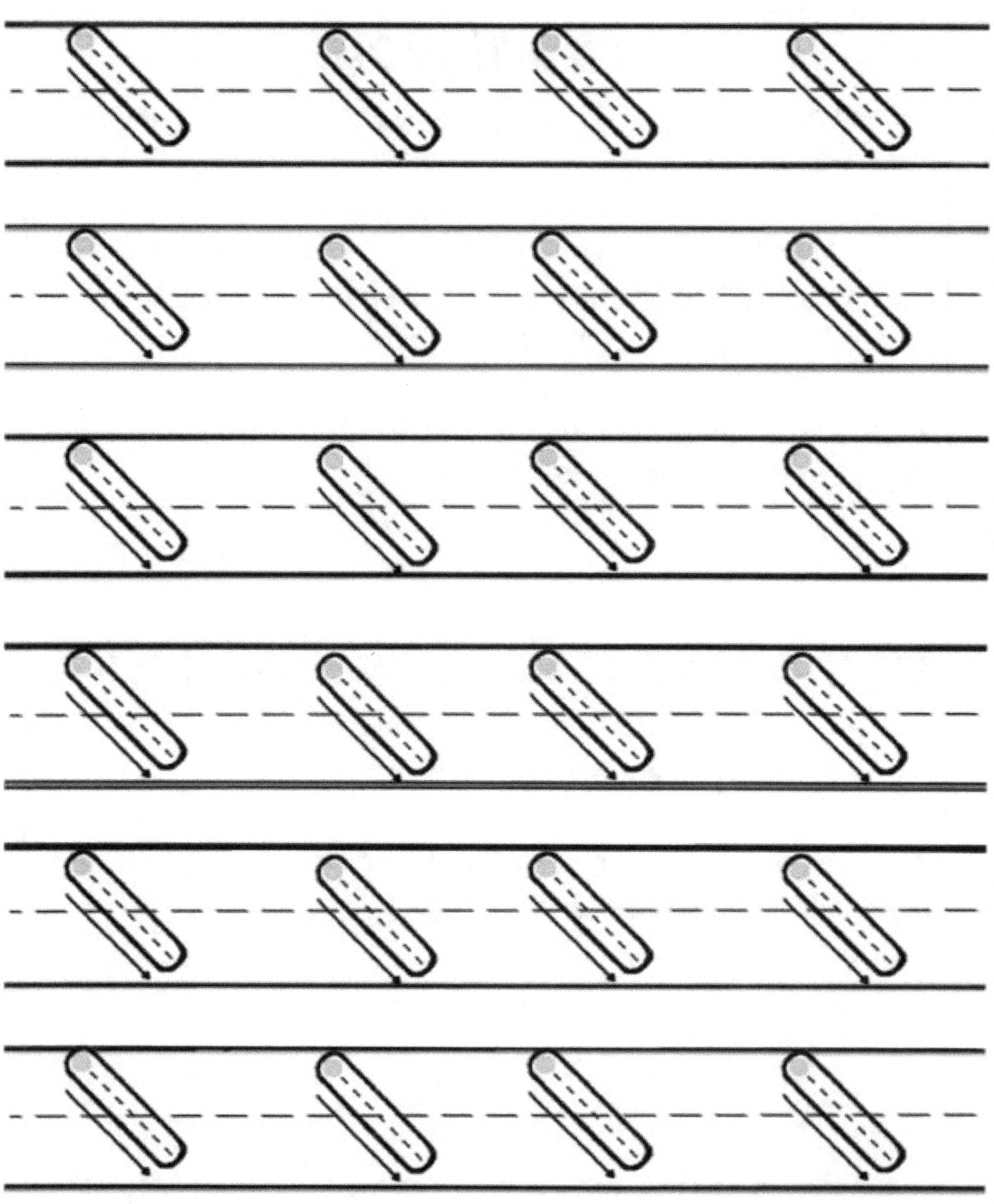

Start at the dot. Trace the dotted line. Use the arrow as a guide

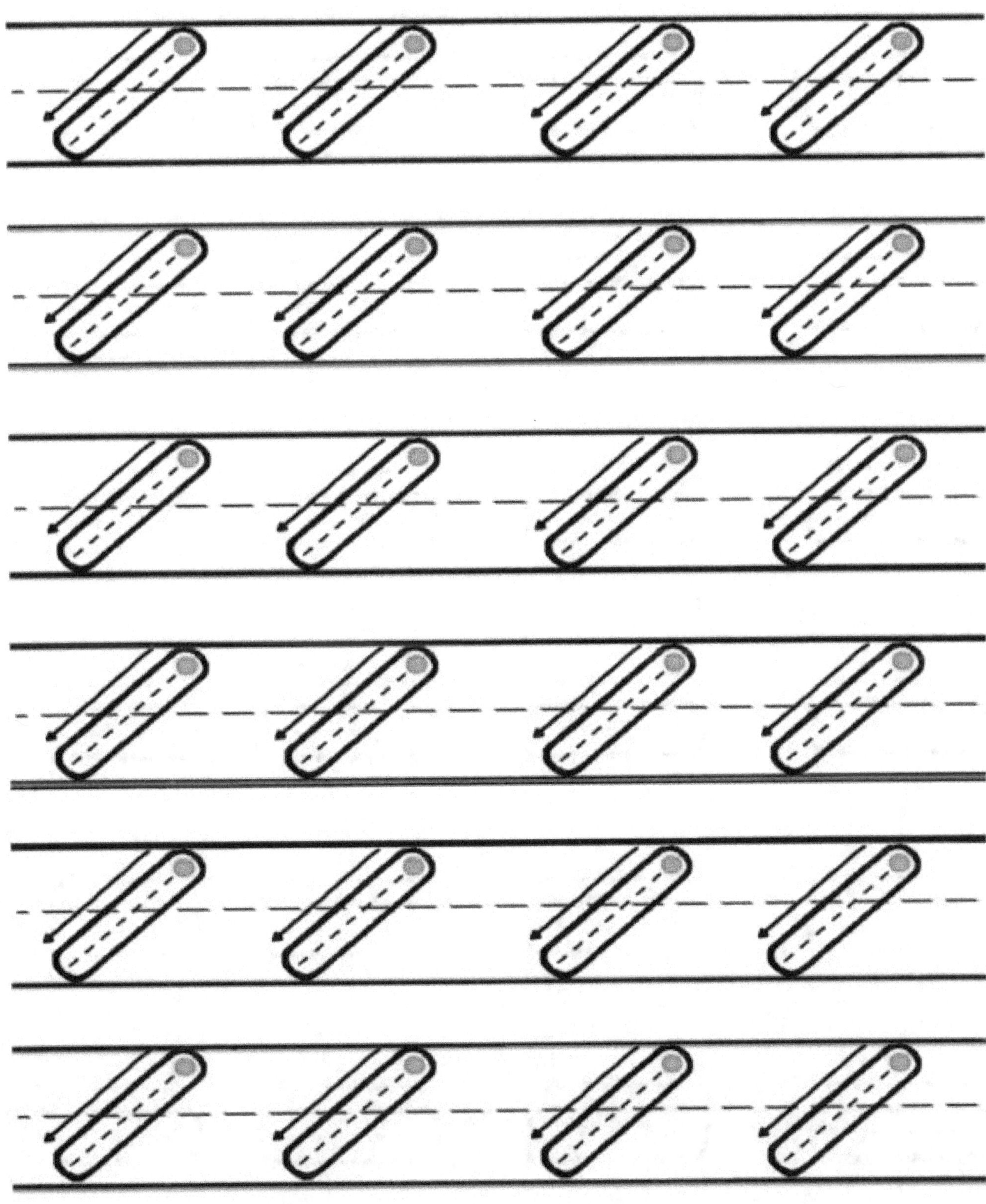

Start at the dot.Trace the dotted line.
Use the arrow as a guide

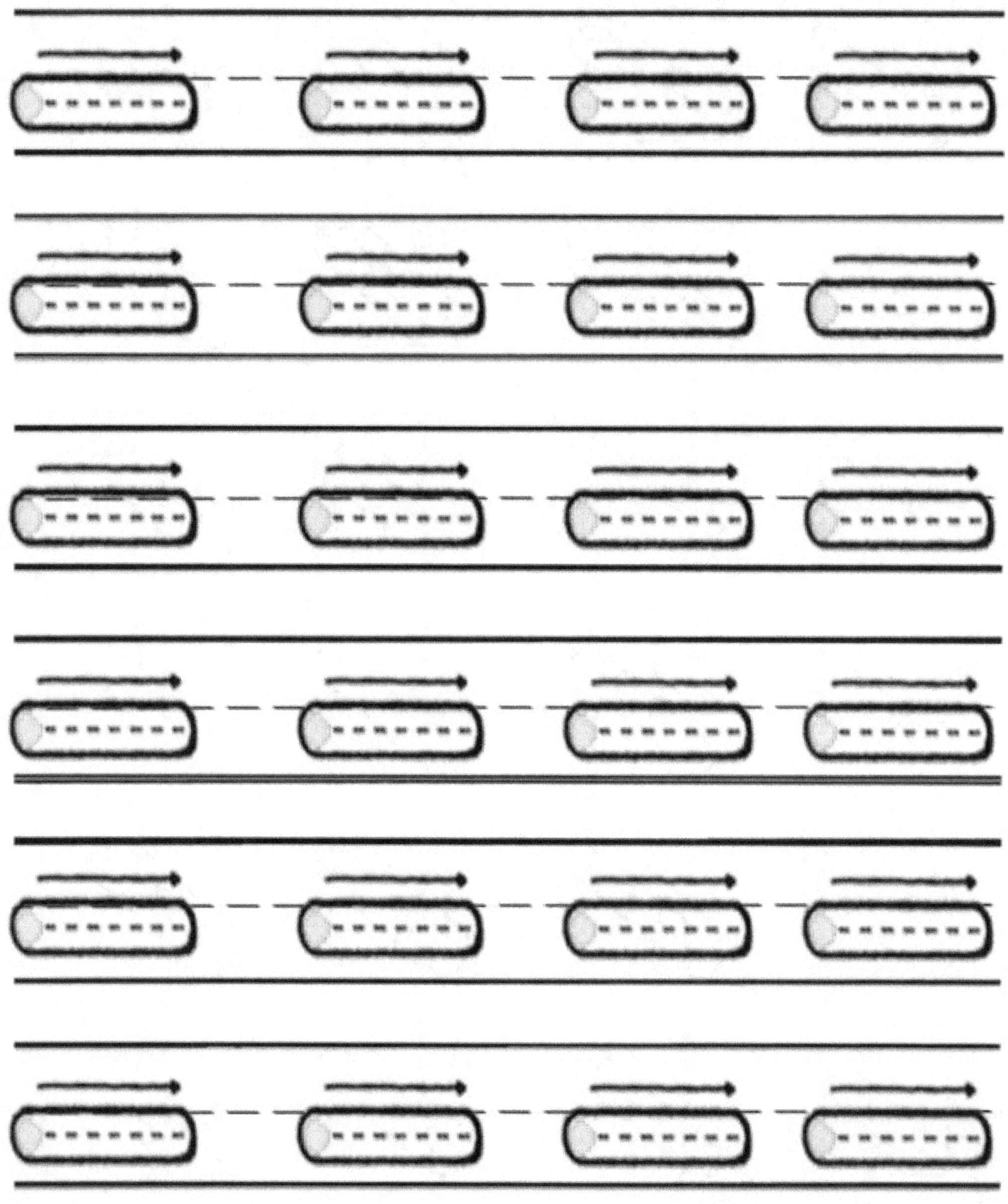

start at the dot.Trace the dotted line.
Use the arrow as a guide

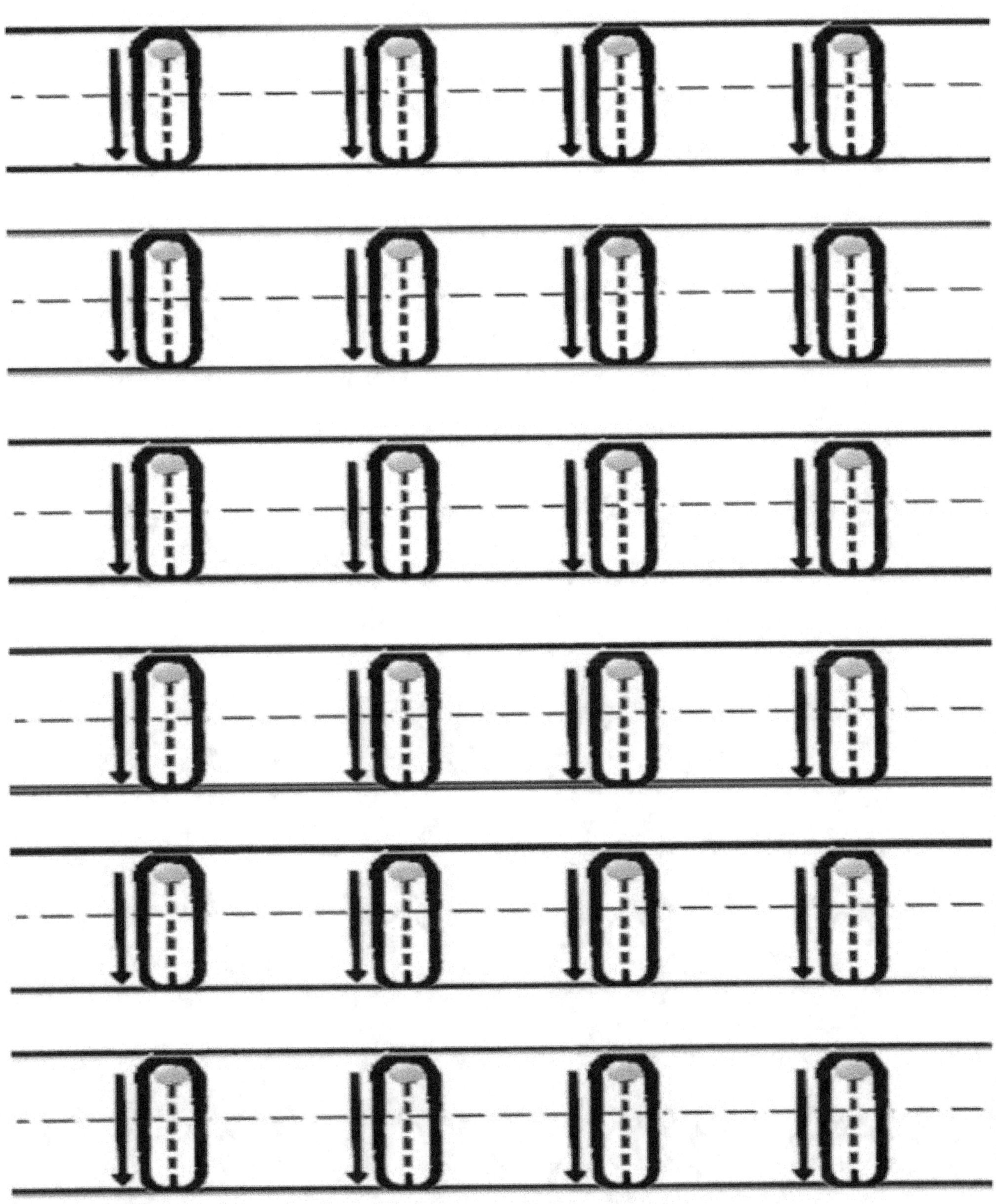

Start at the dot. Trace the dotted line. Use the arrow as a guide

Start at the dot. Trace the dotted line. Use the arrow as a guide

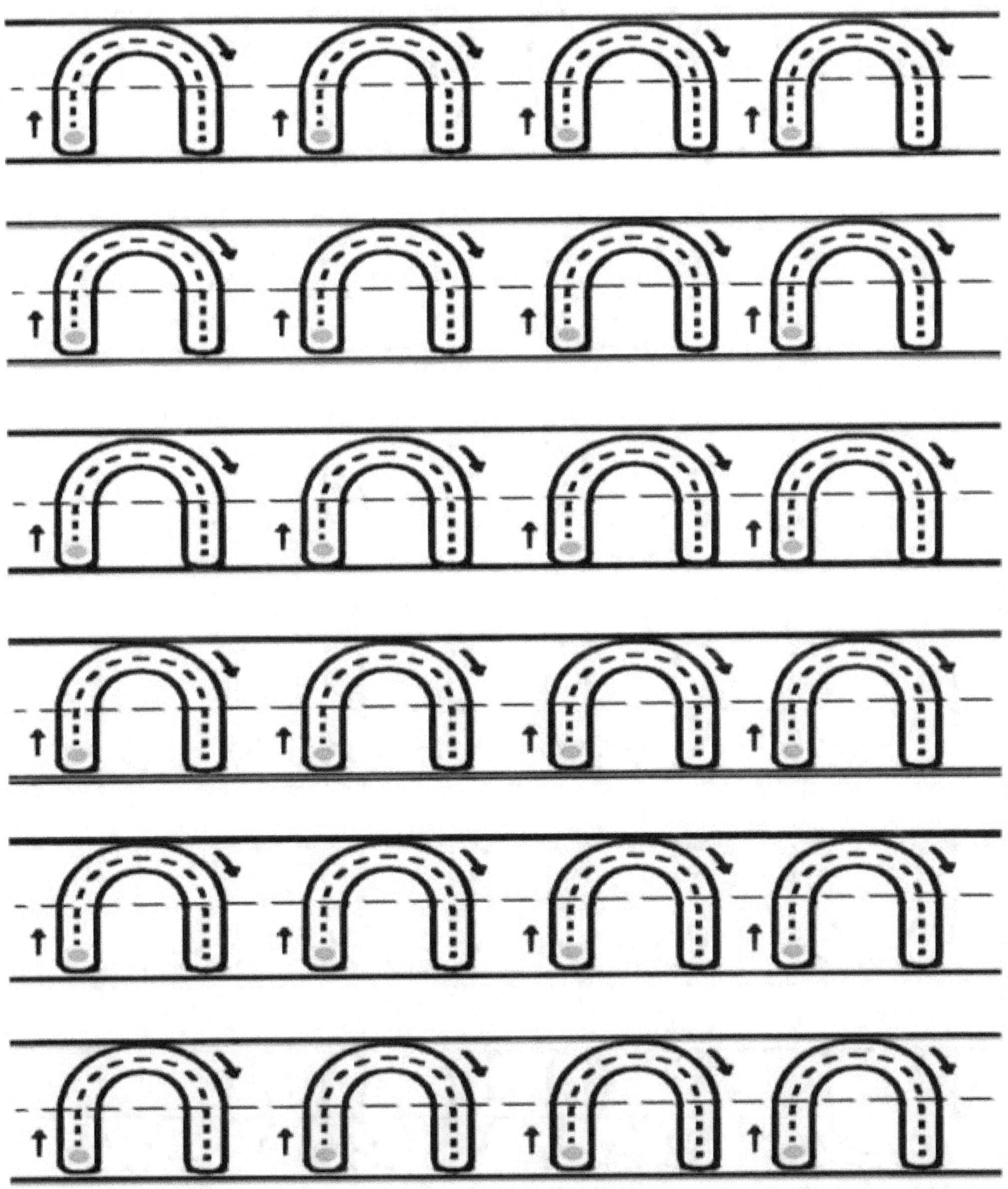

Start at the dot. Trace the dotted line.
Use the arrow as a guide

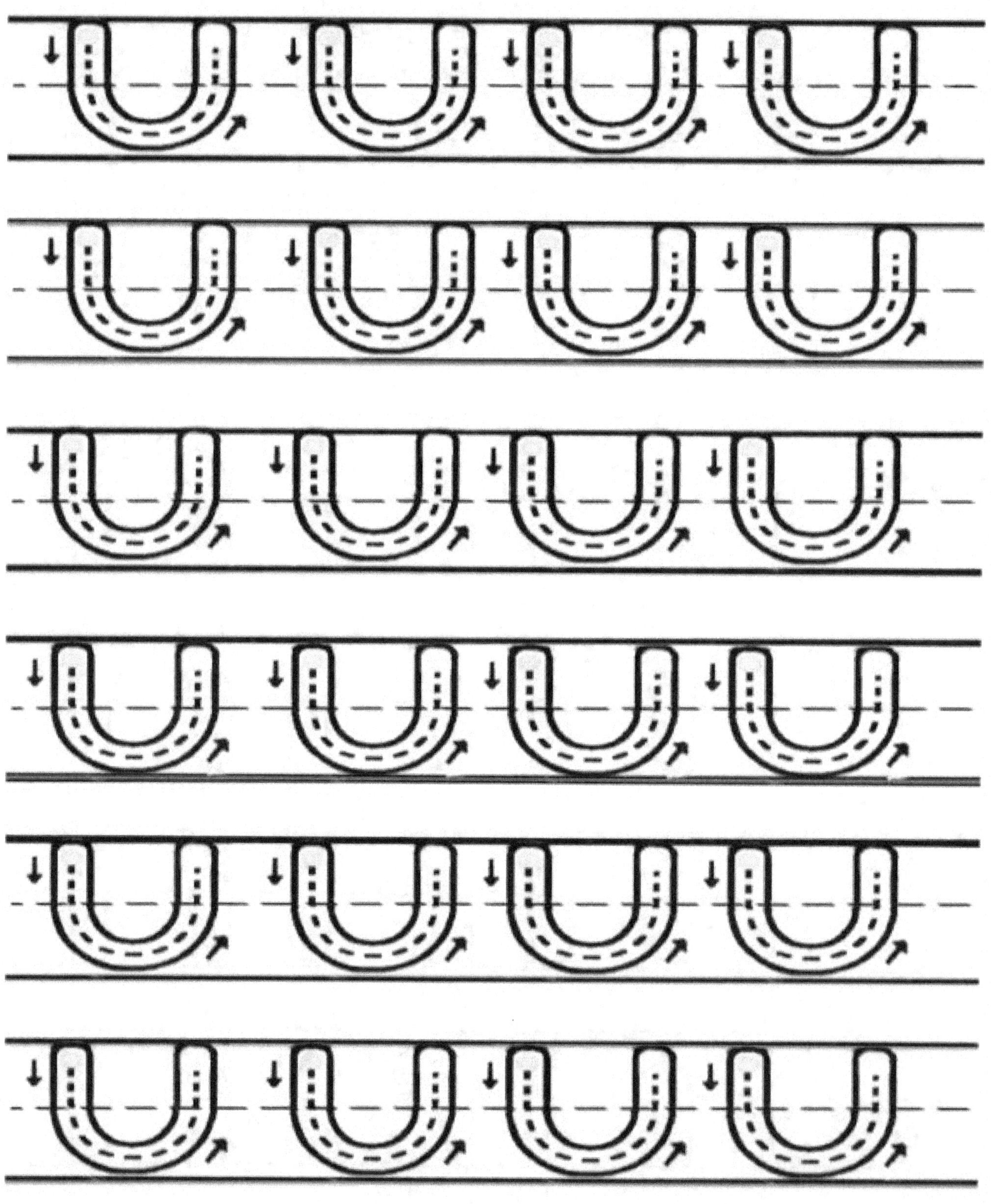

start at the dot.Trace the dotted line.
Use the arrow as a guide

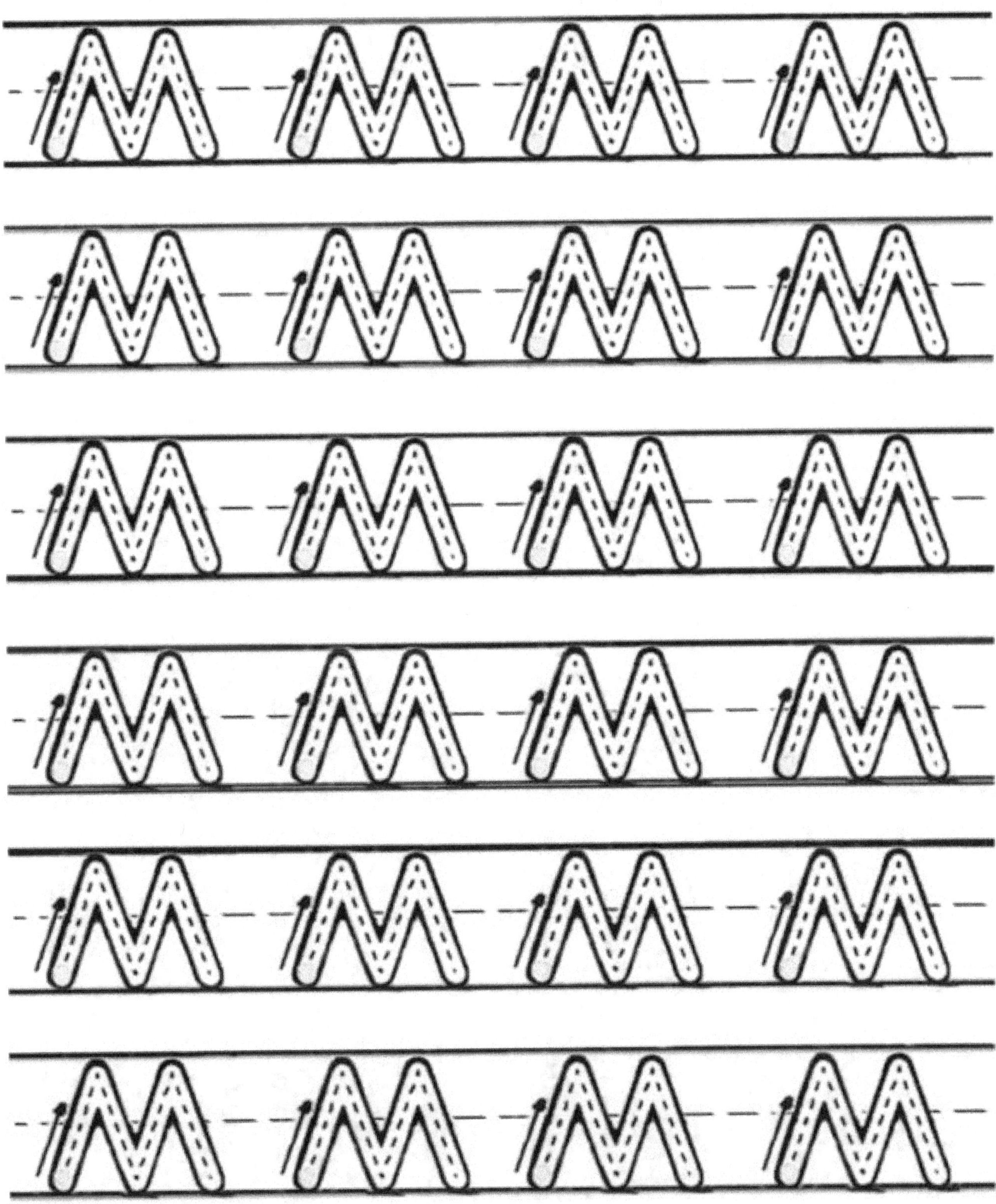

Start at the dot.Trace the dotted line. Use the arrow as a guide

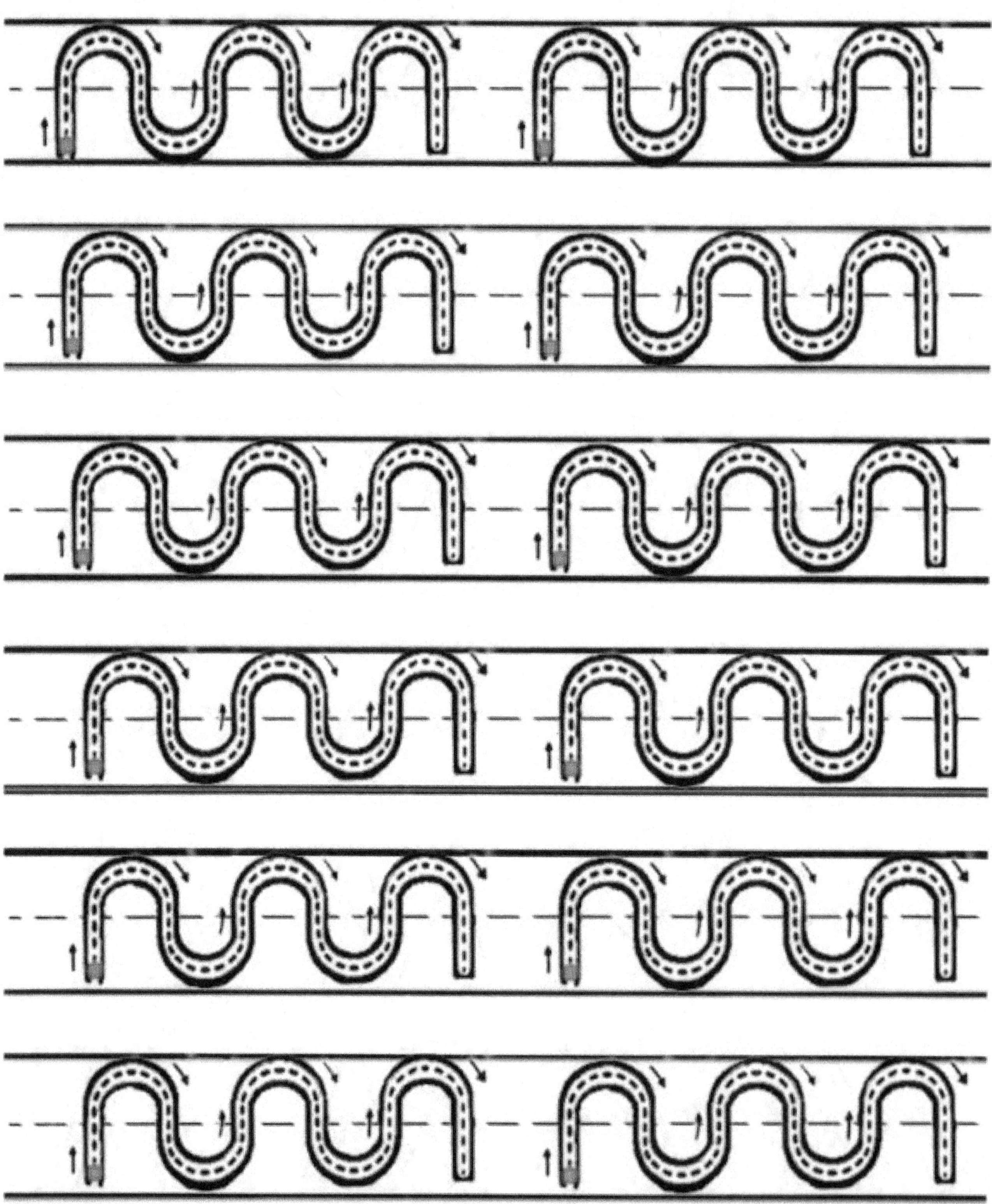

A is for

The Letter A

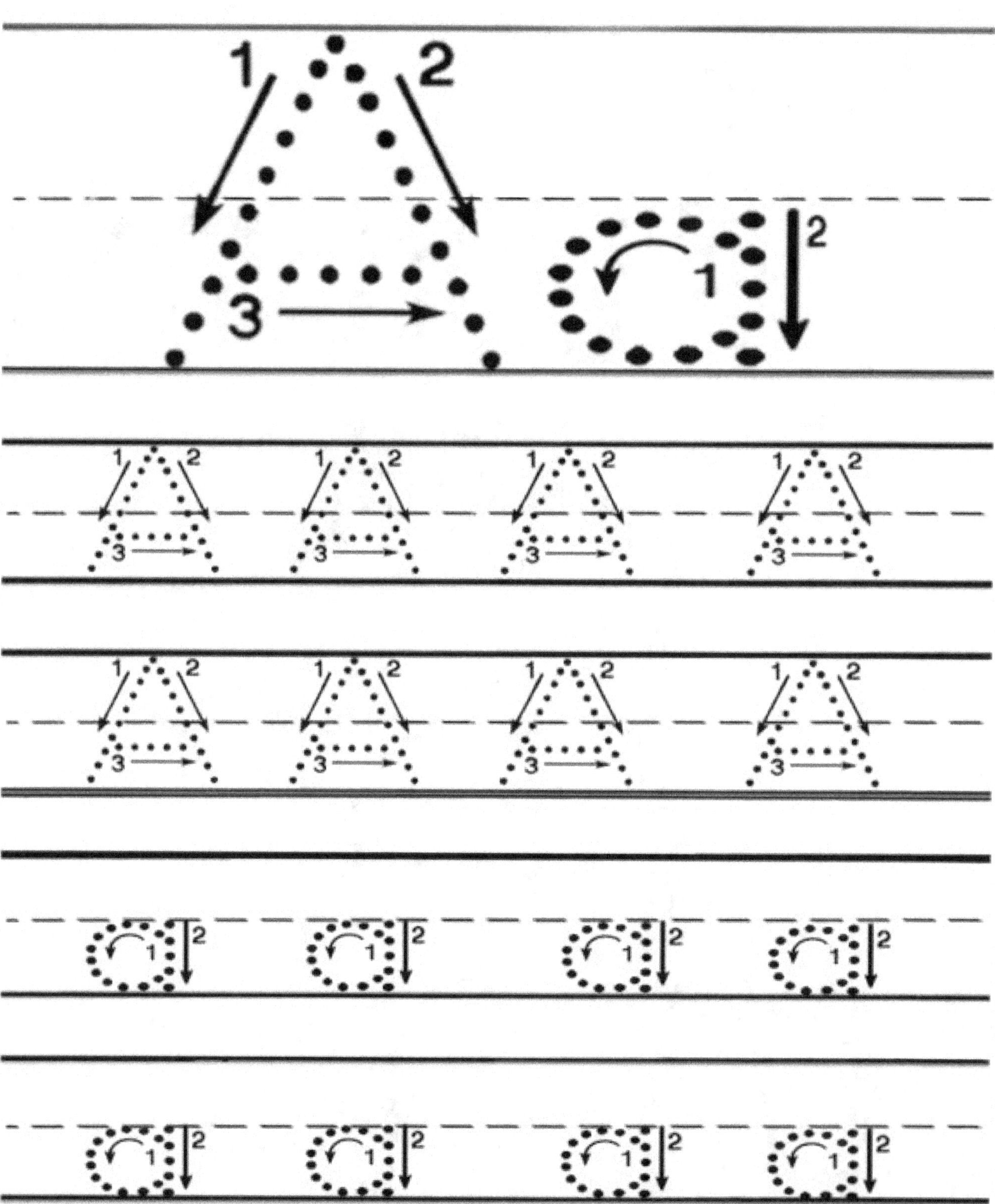

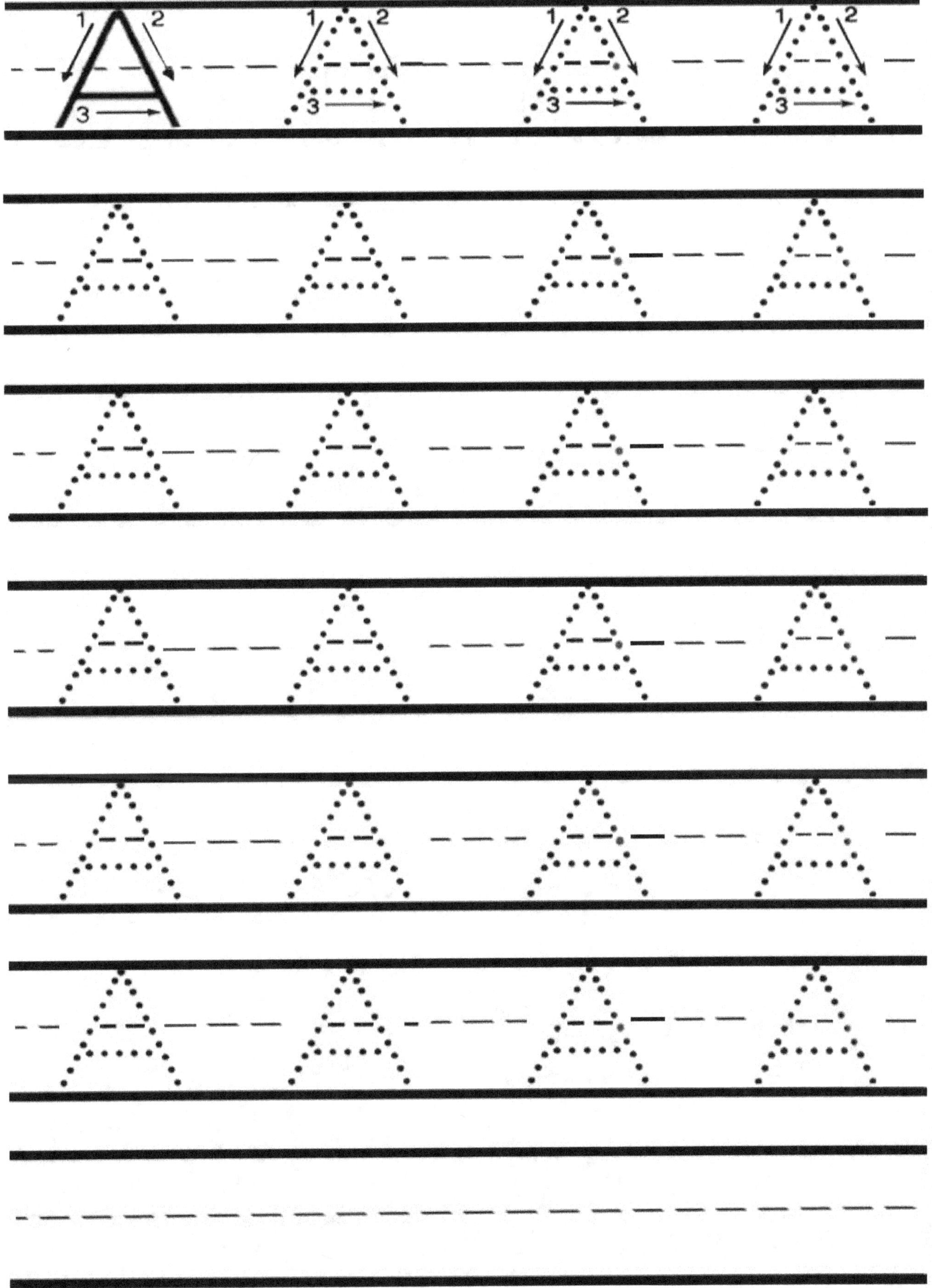

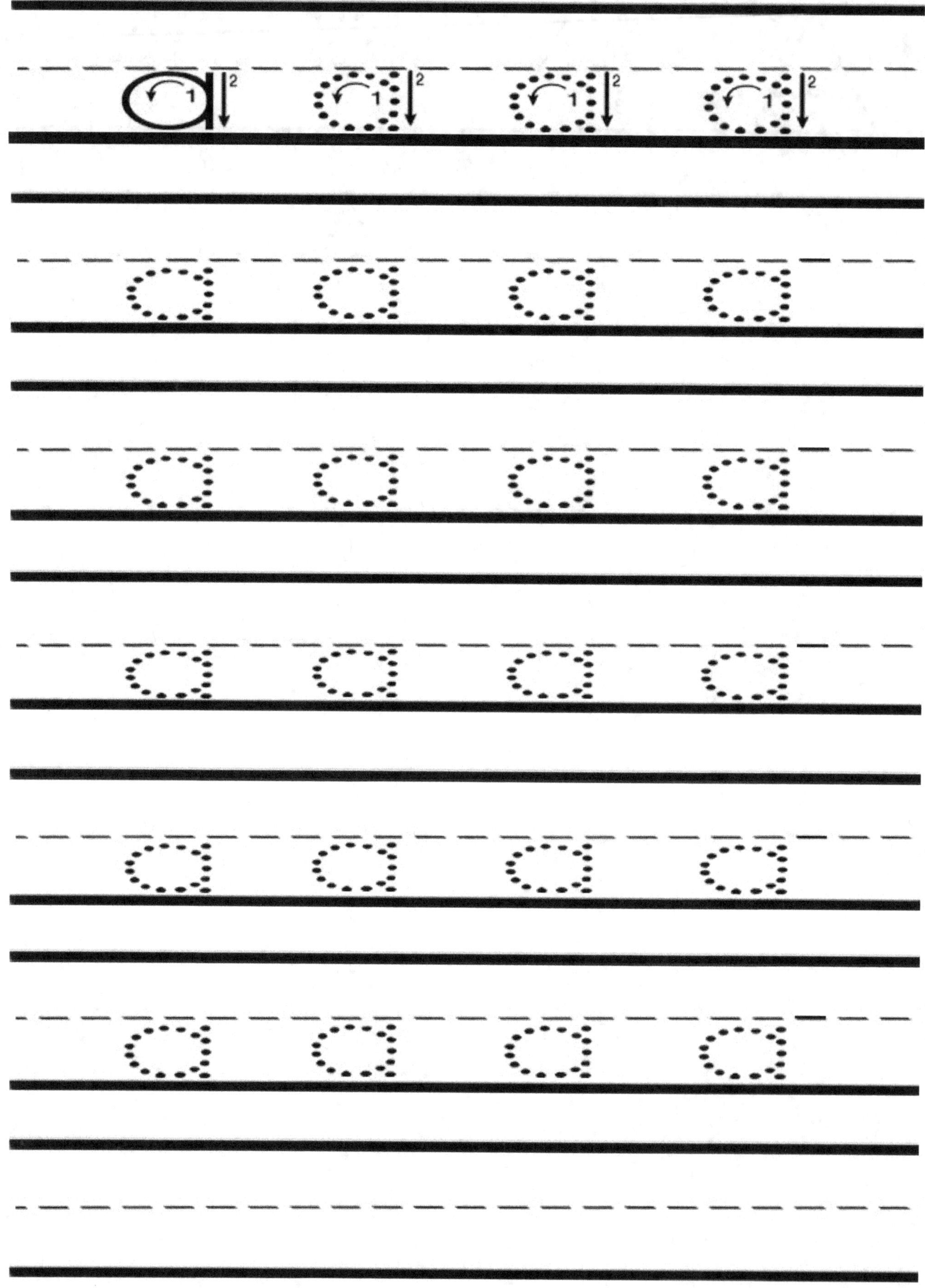

B is for

The Letter B

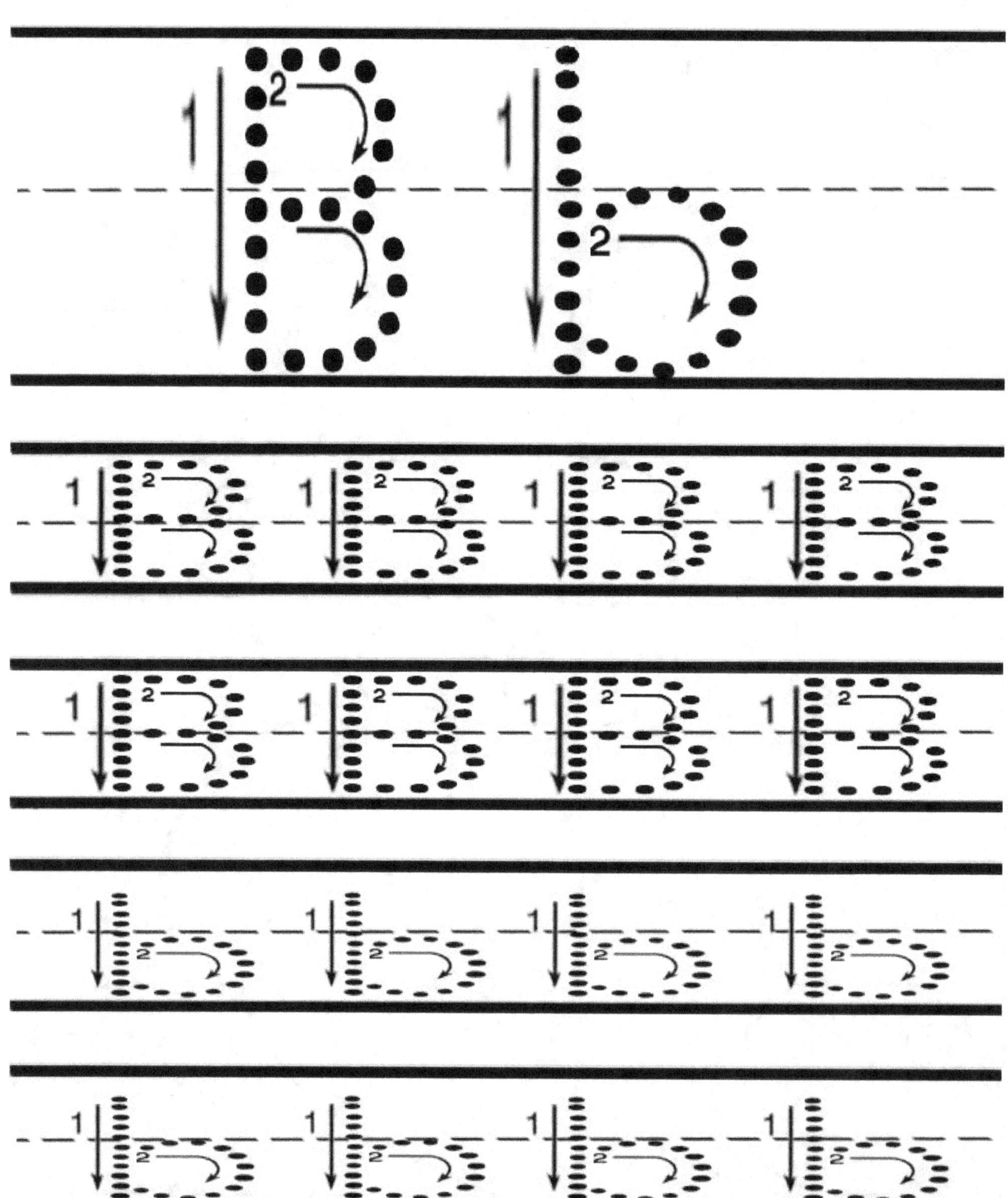

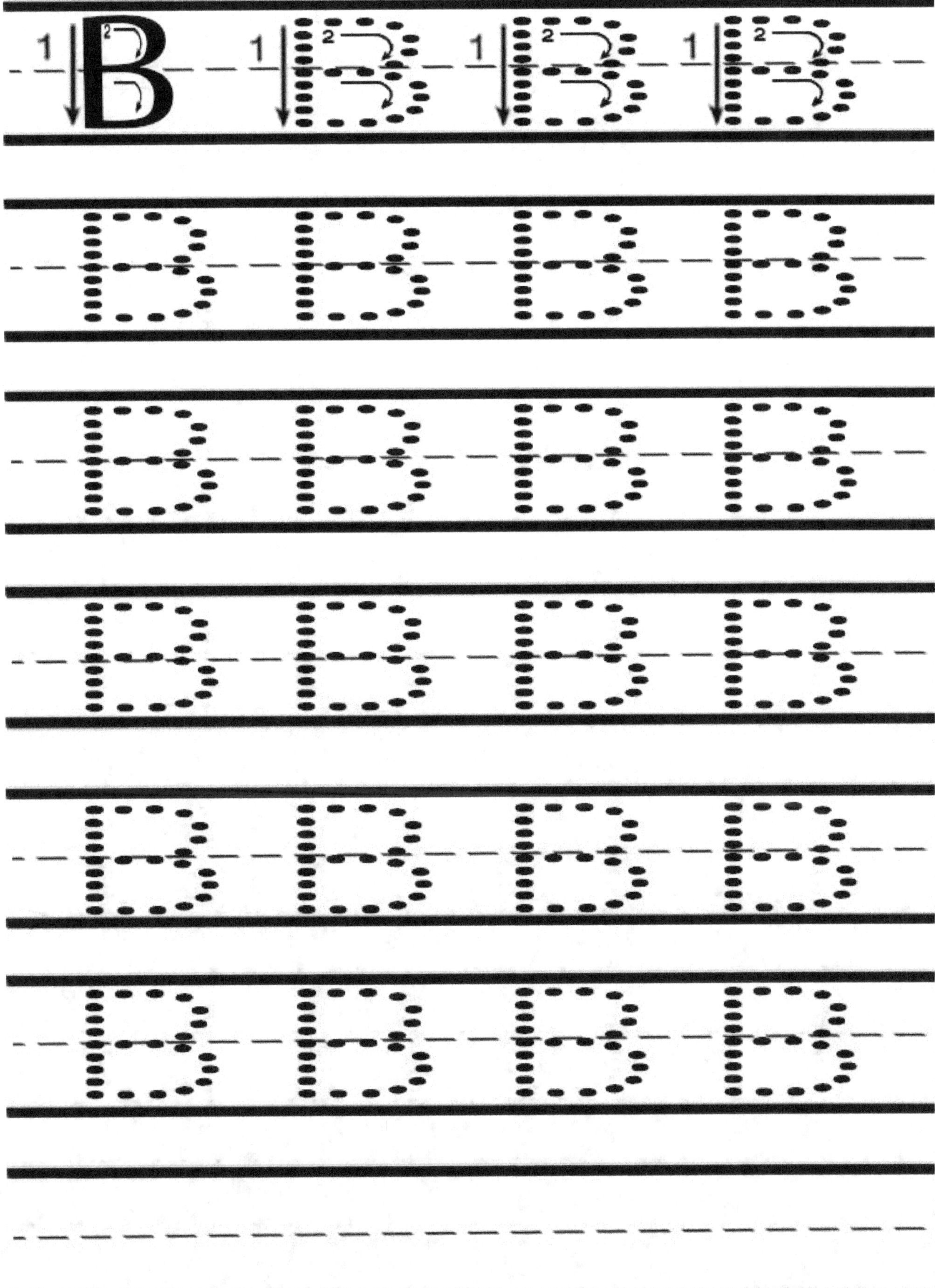

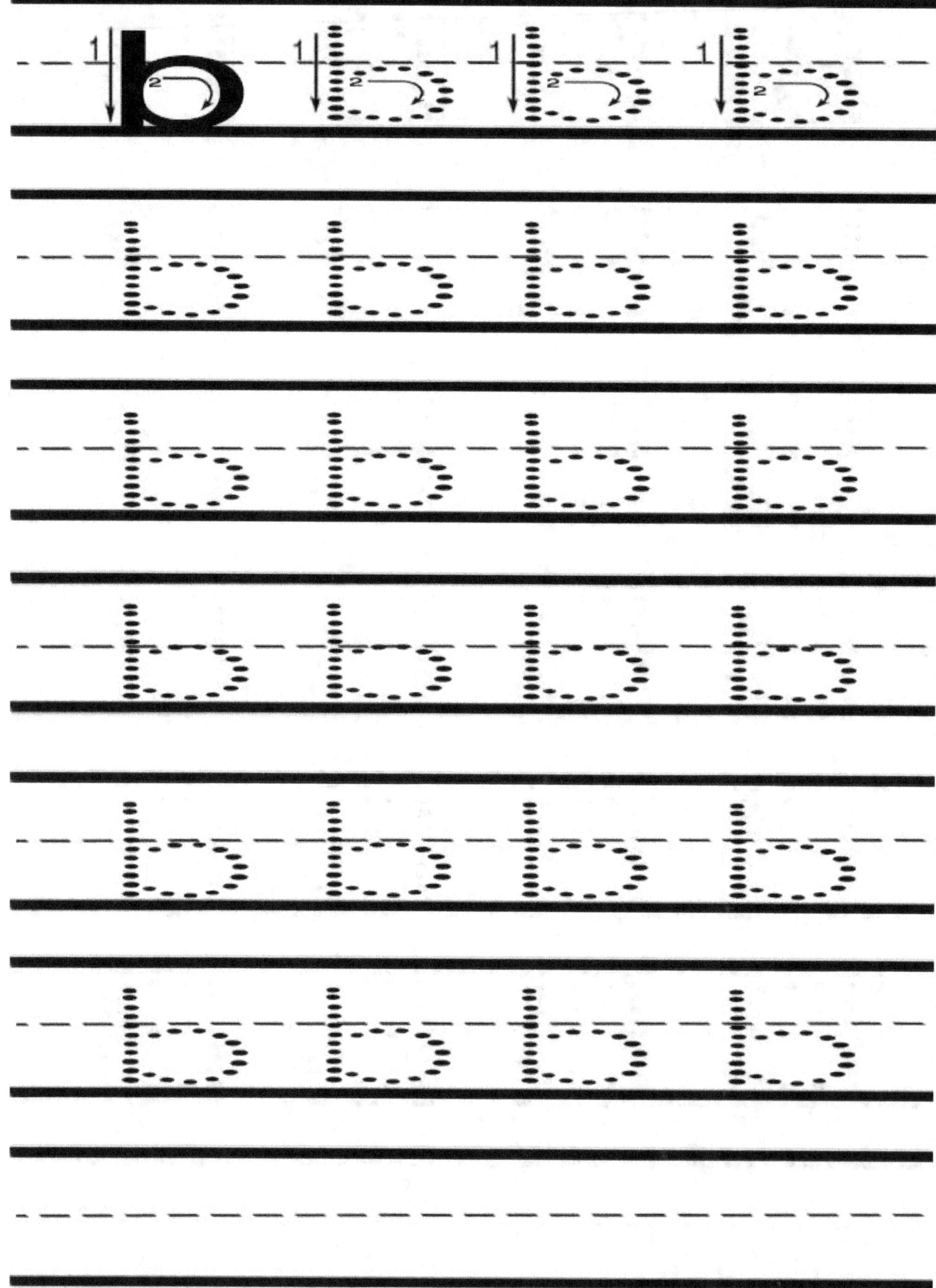

C is for

The Letter C

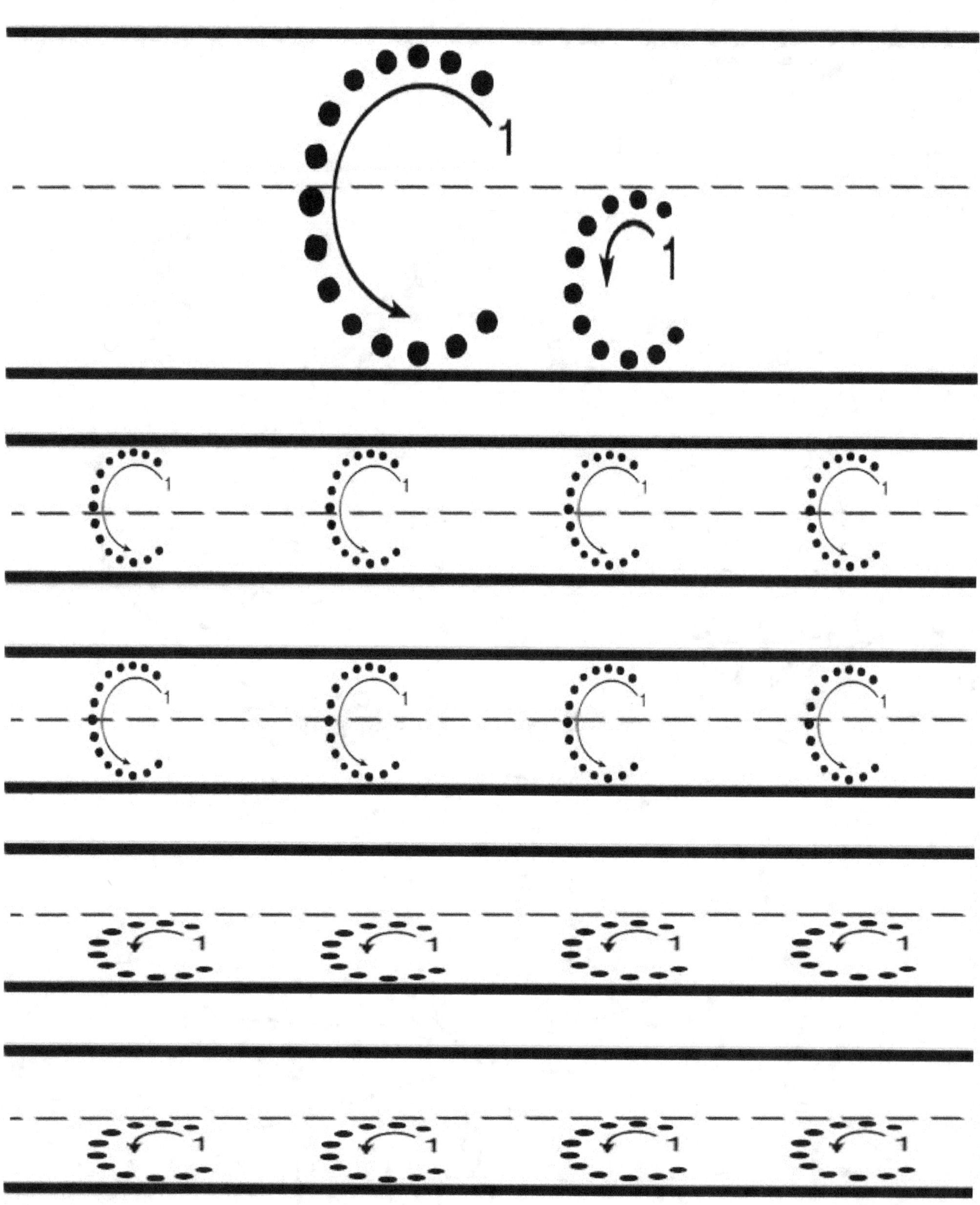

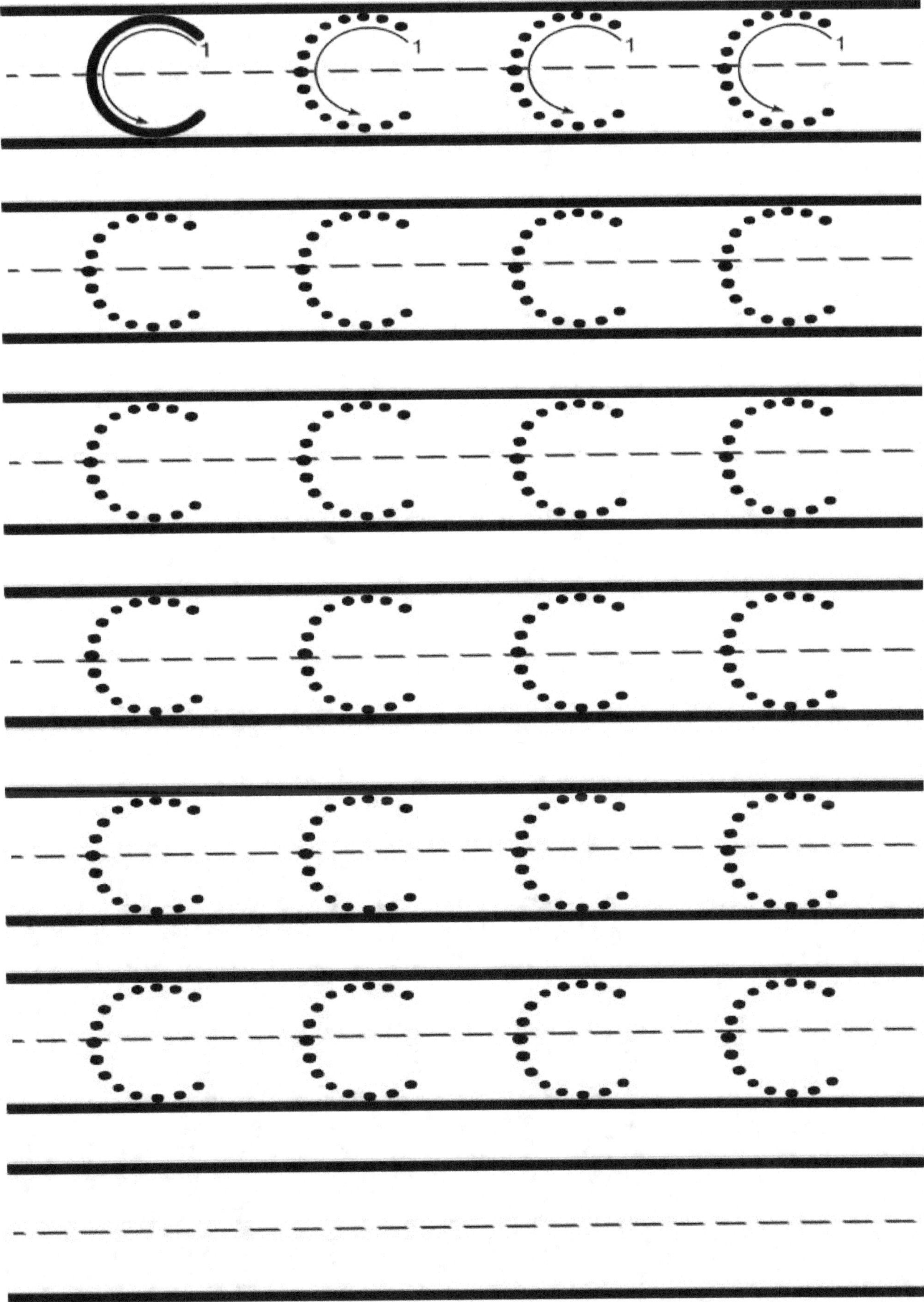

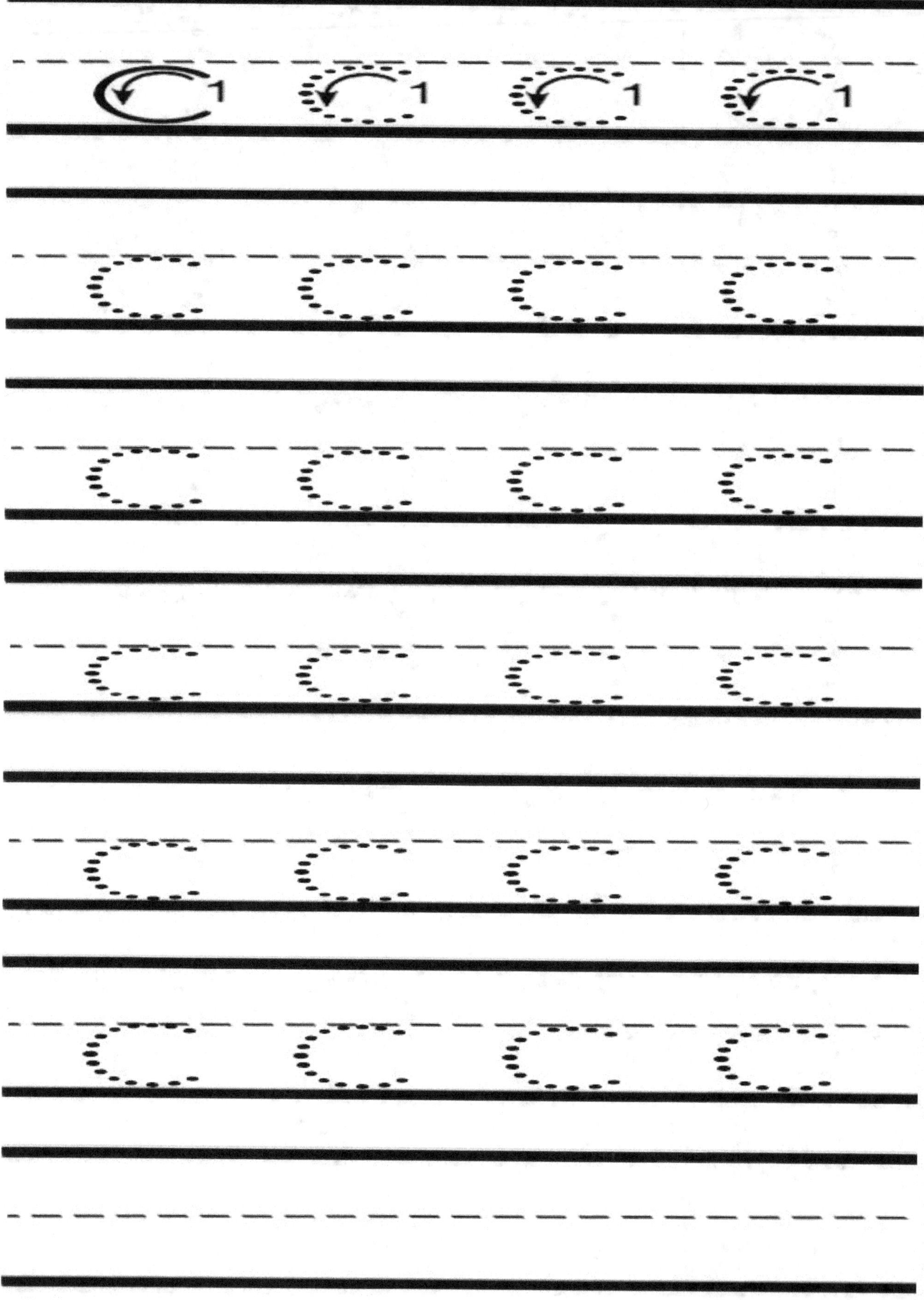

D is for

The Letter D

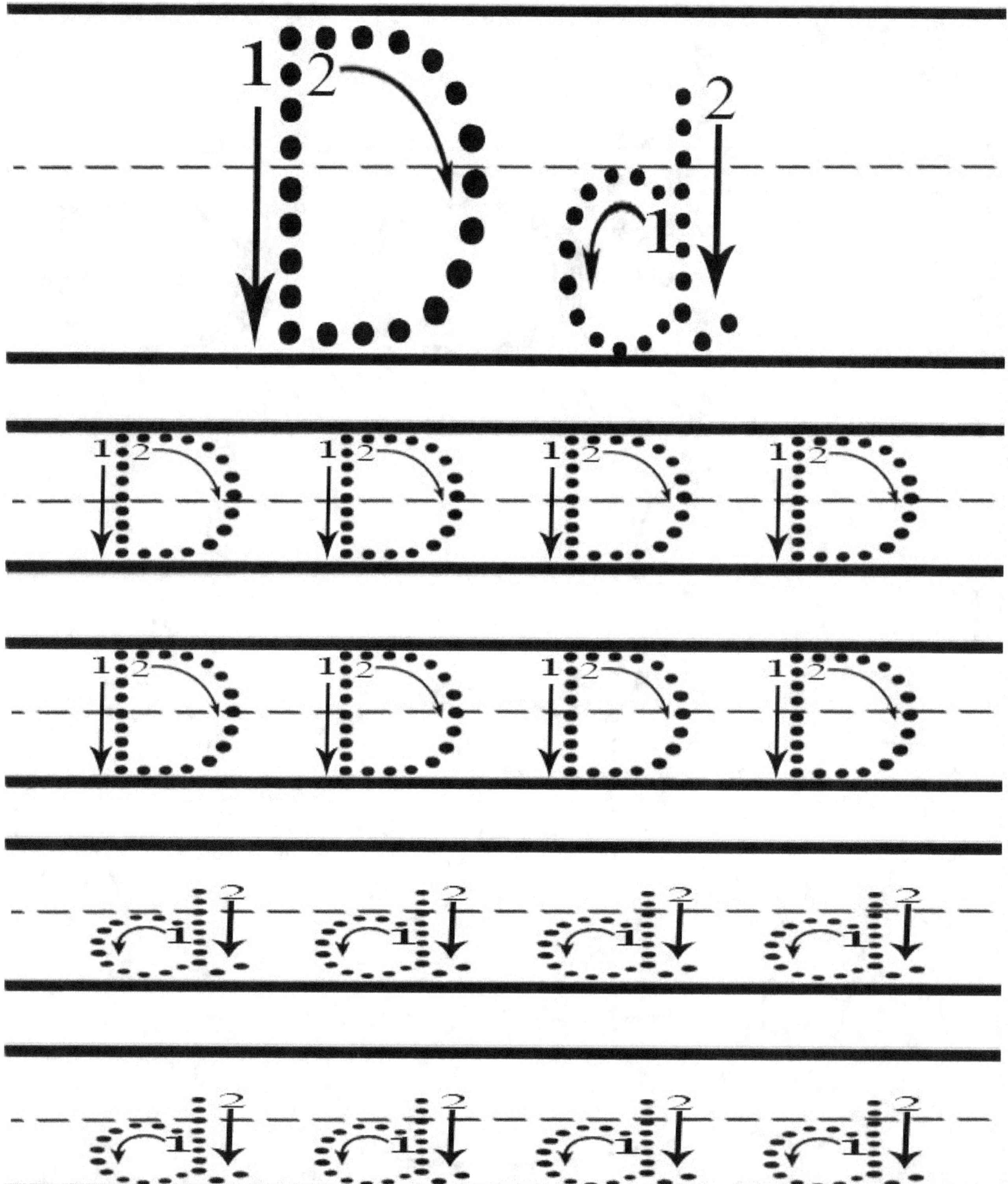

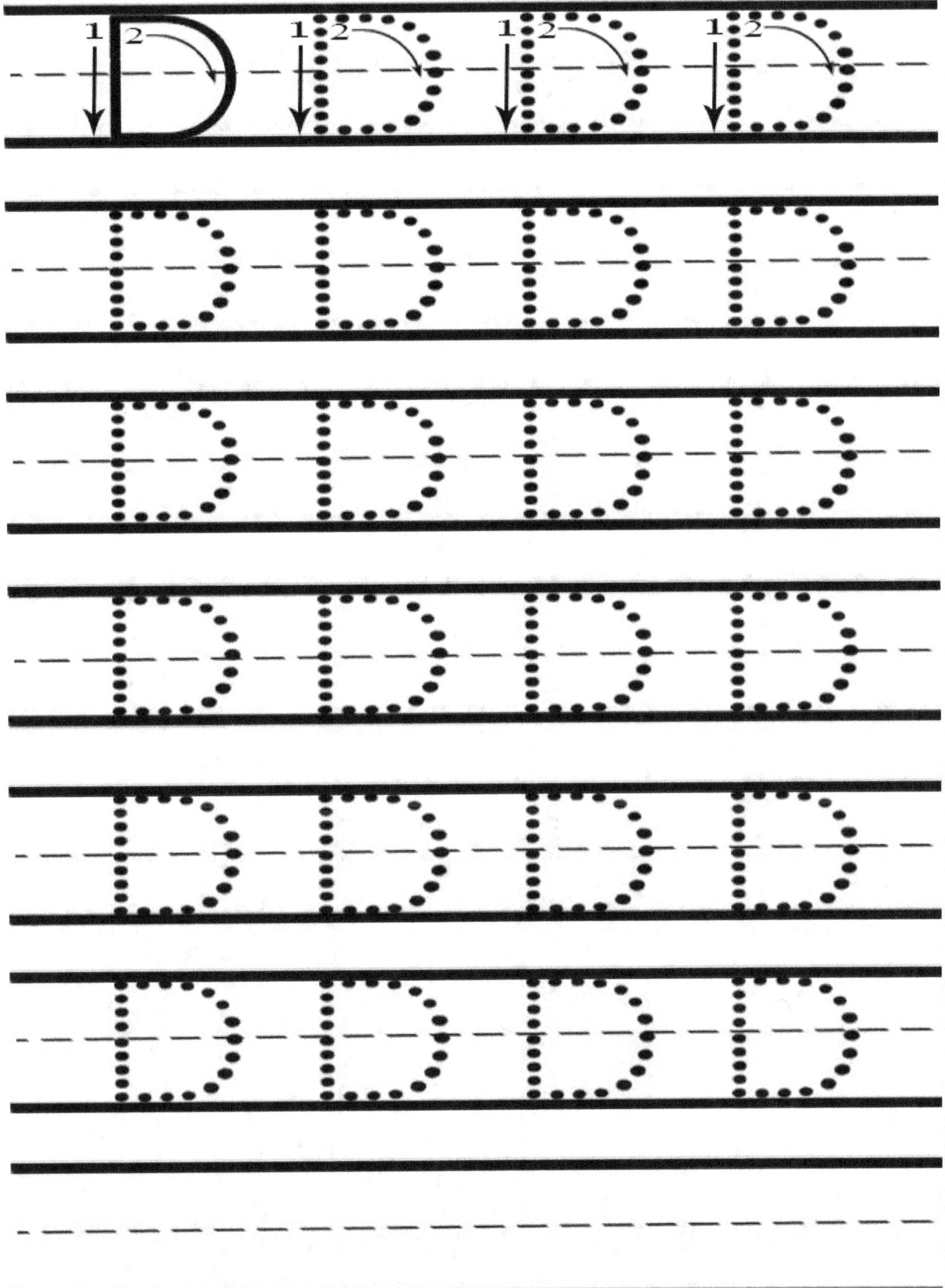

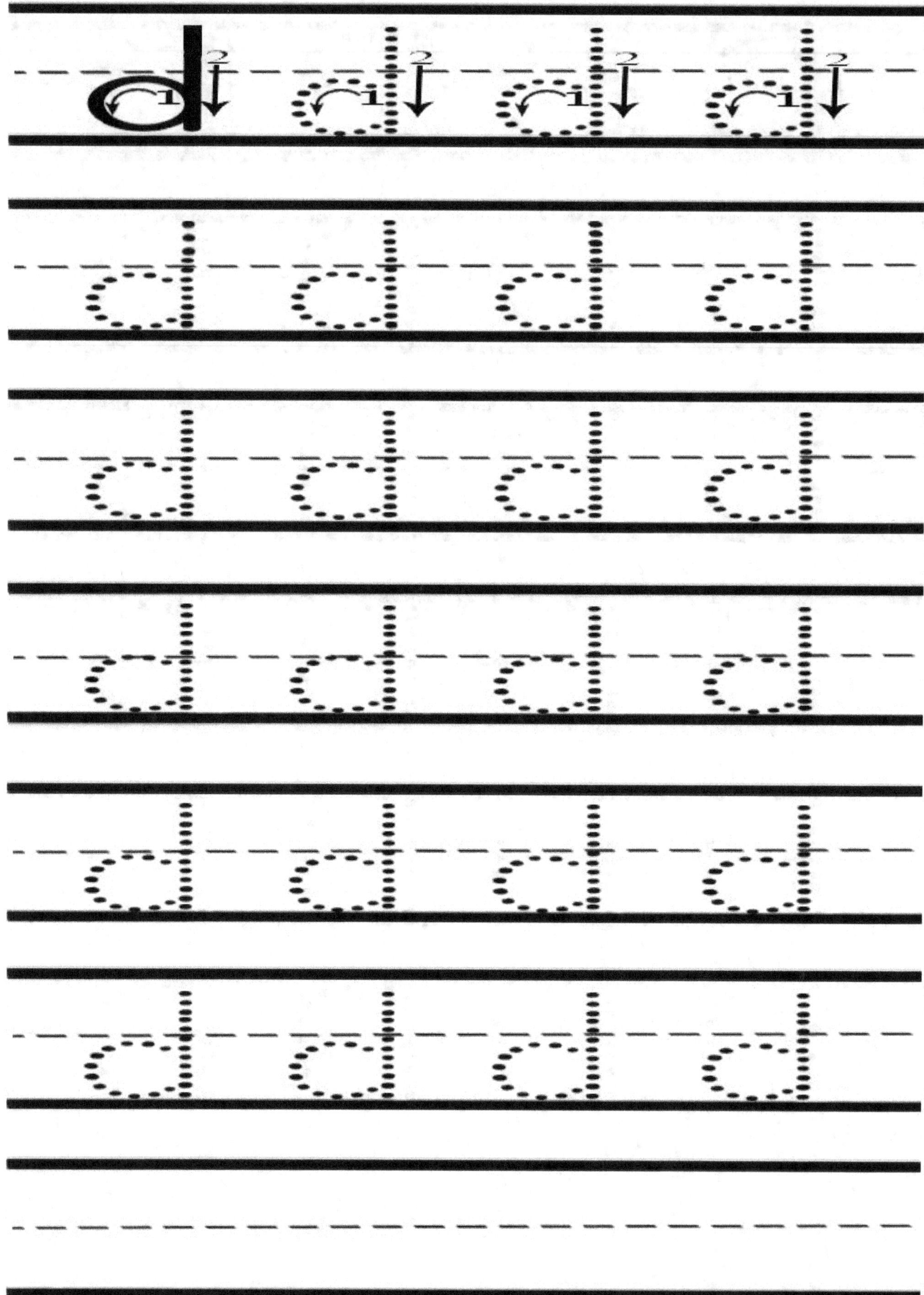

E is for

LEPHANT

The Letter E

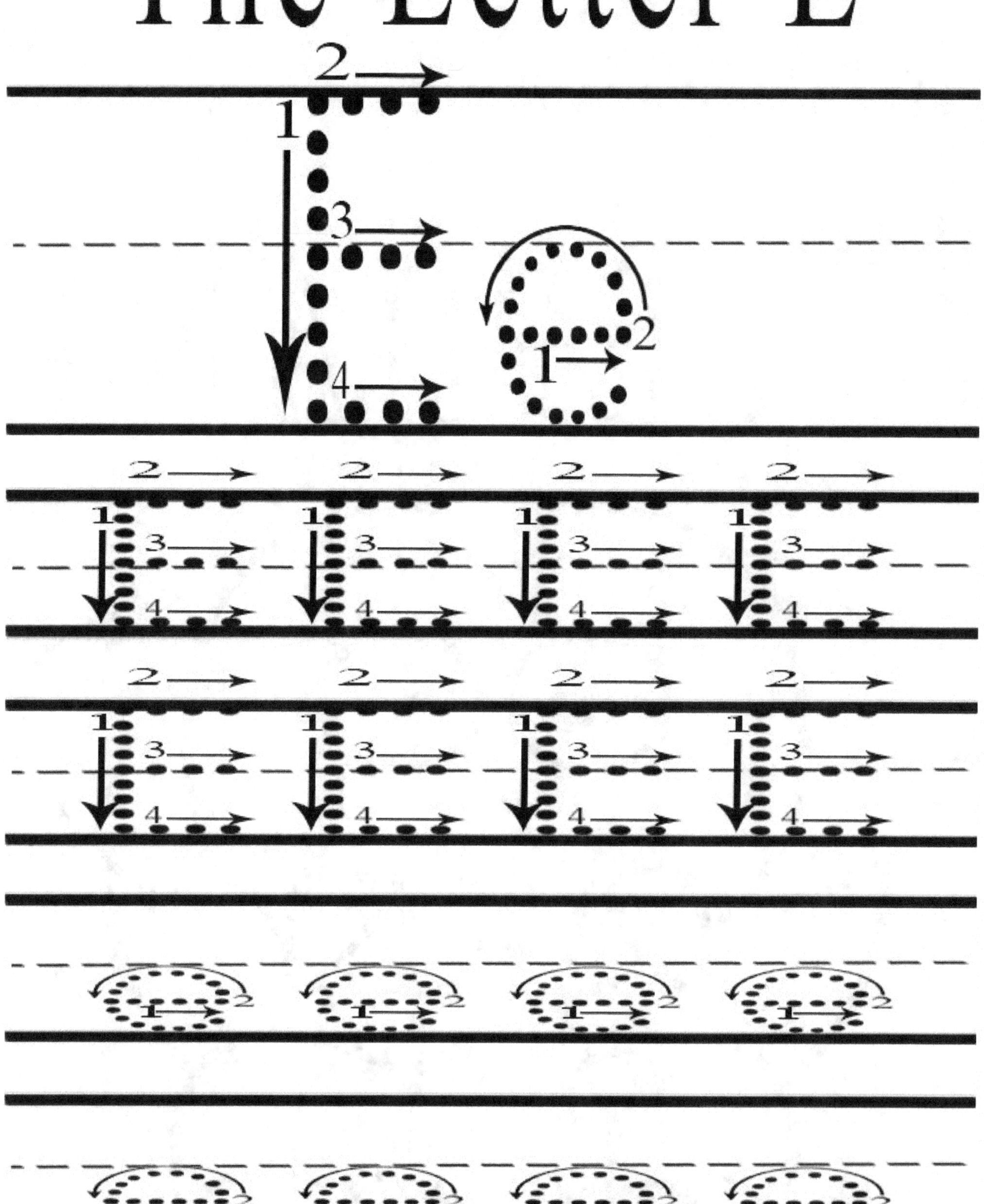

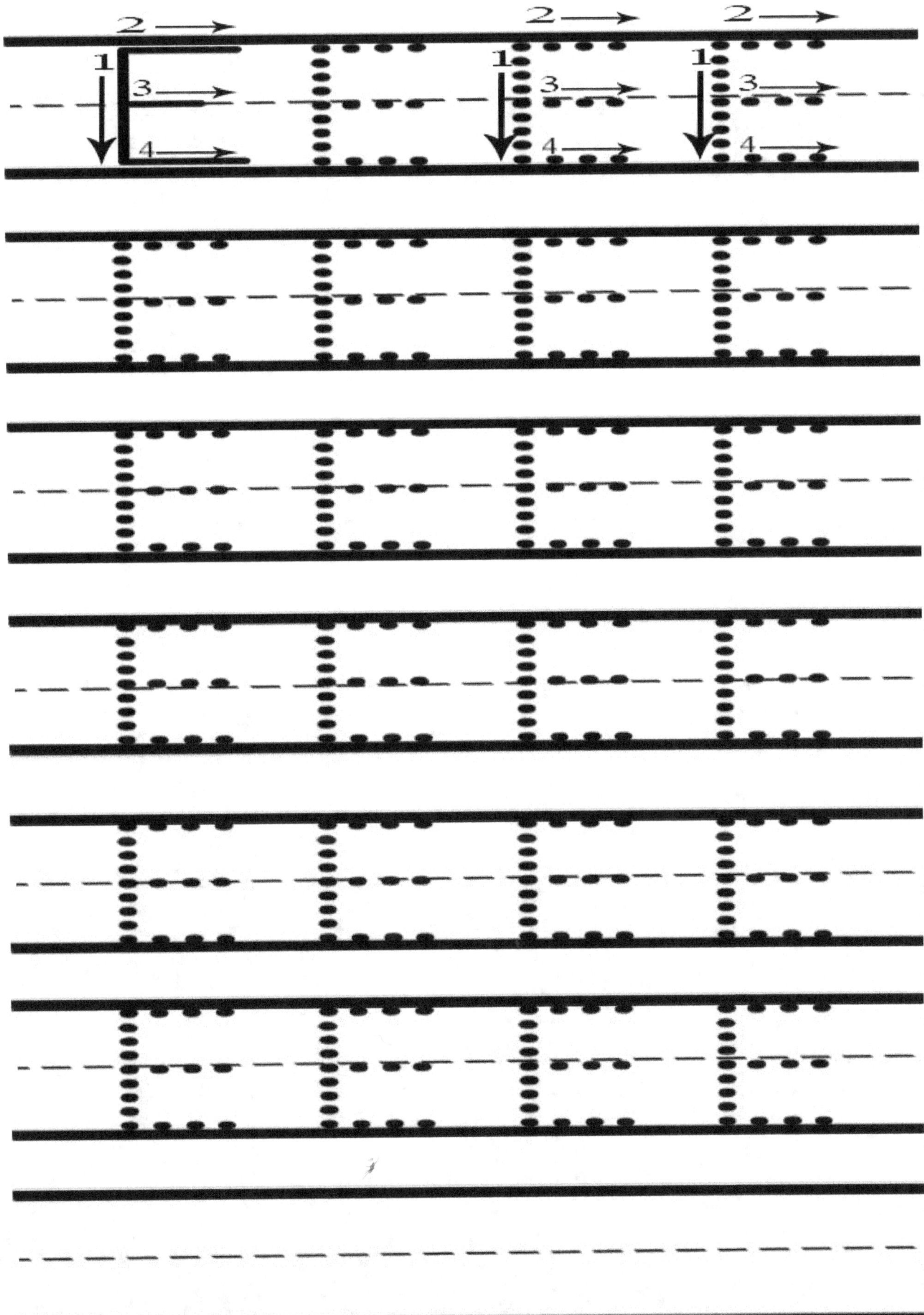

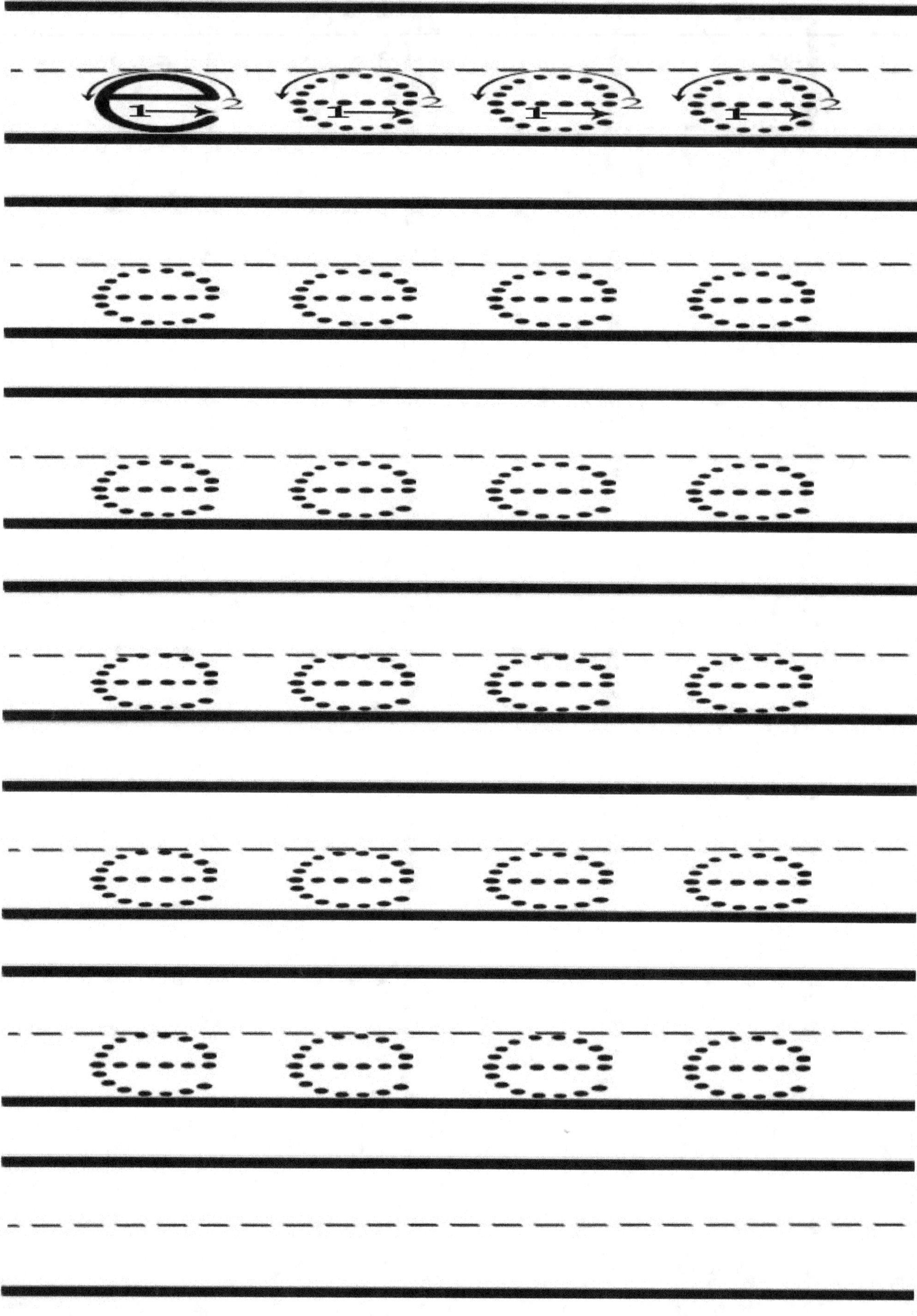

F is for

ISH

The Letter F

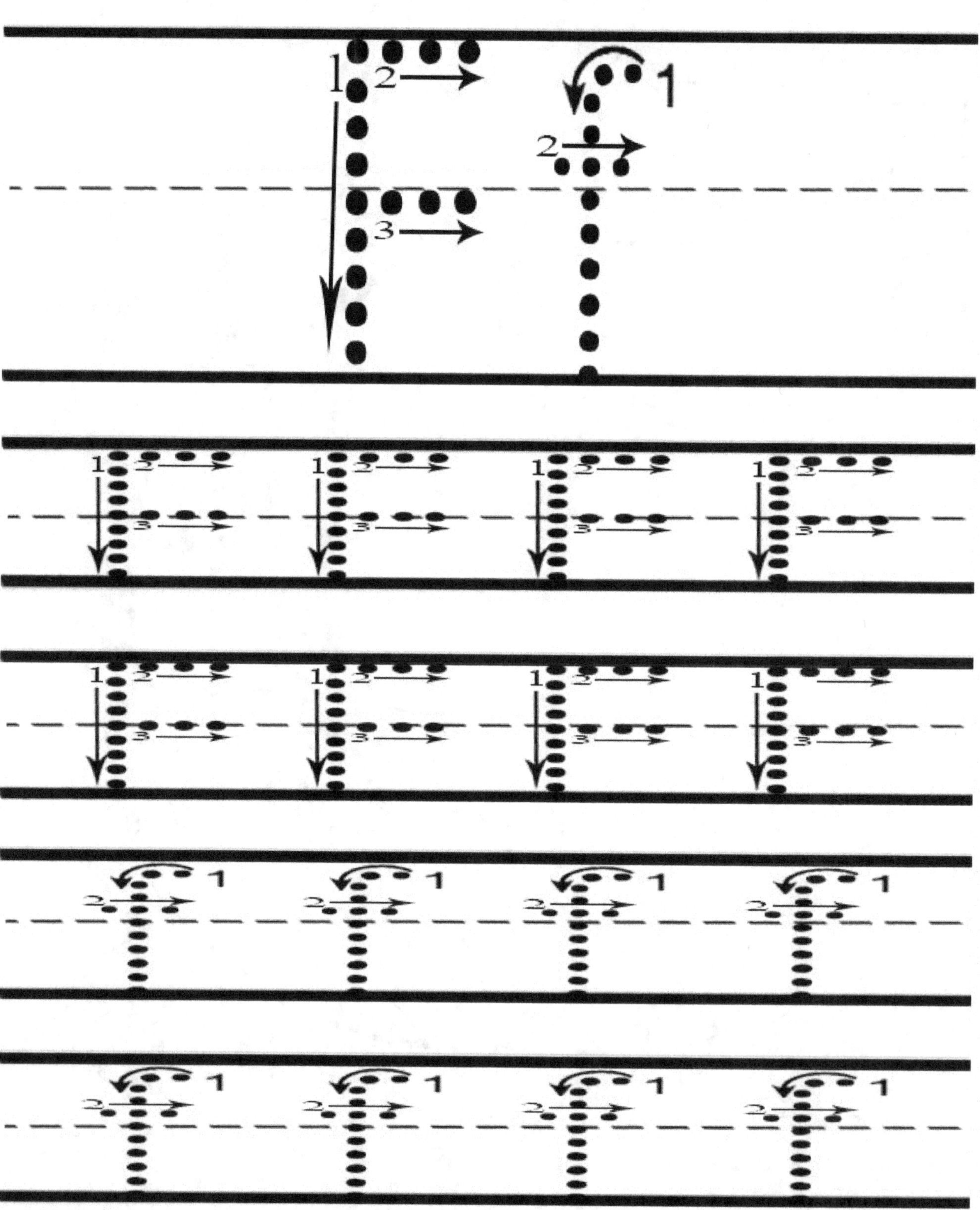

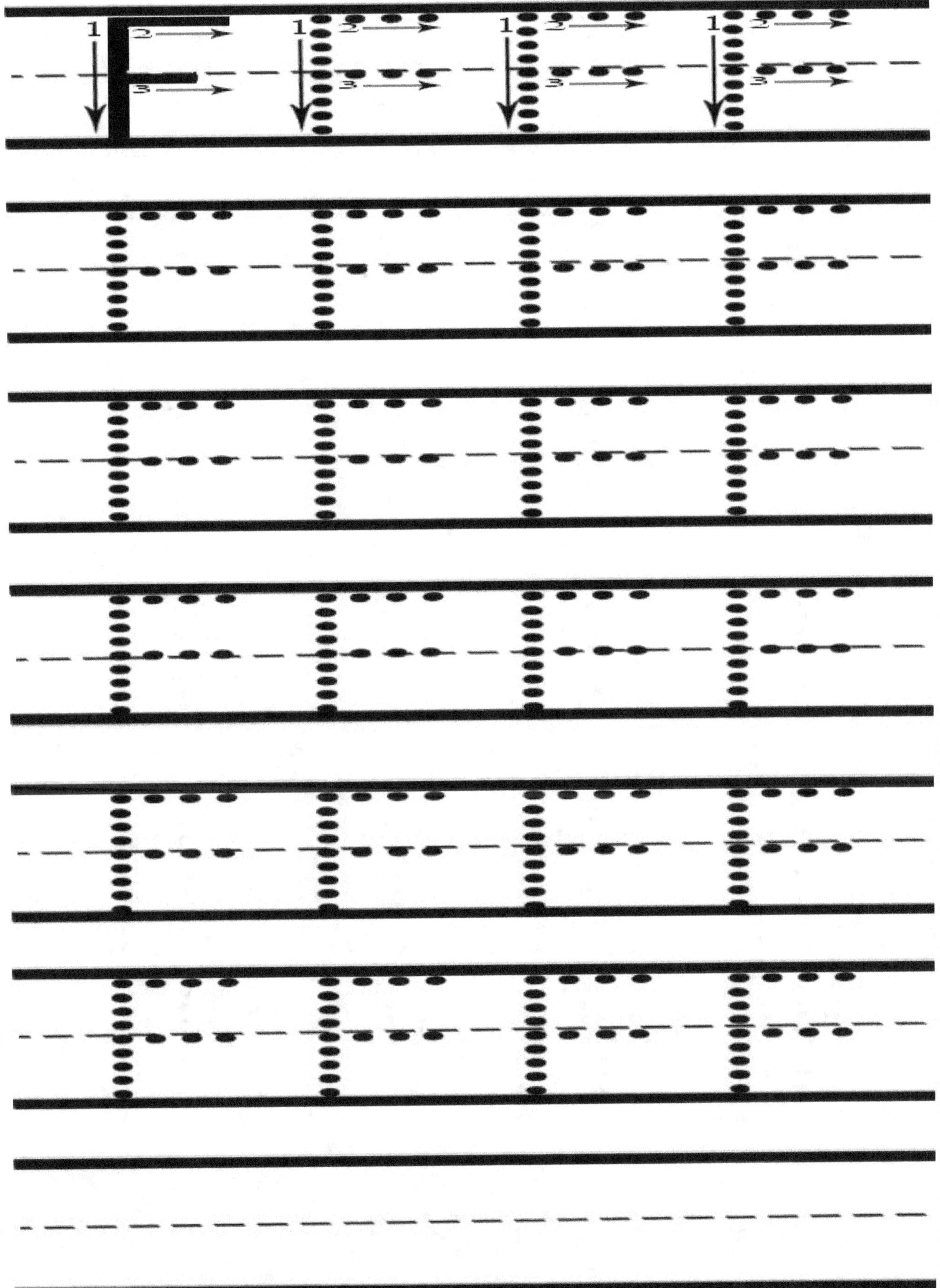

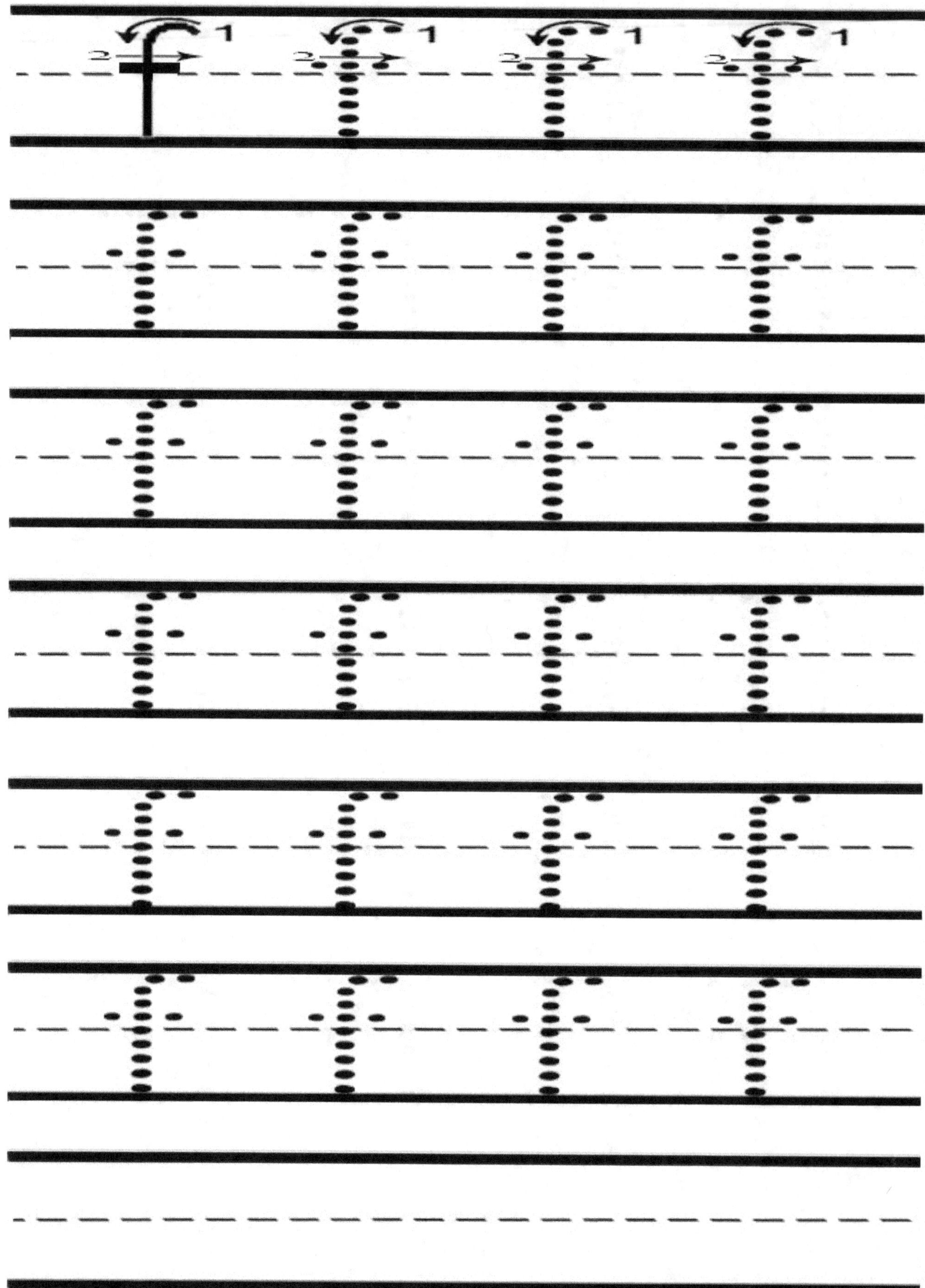

G is for

GIRAFFE

The Letter G

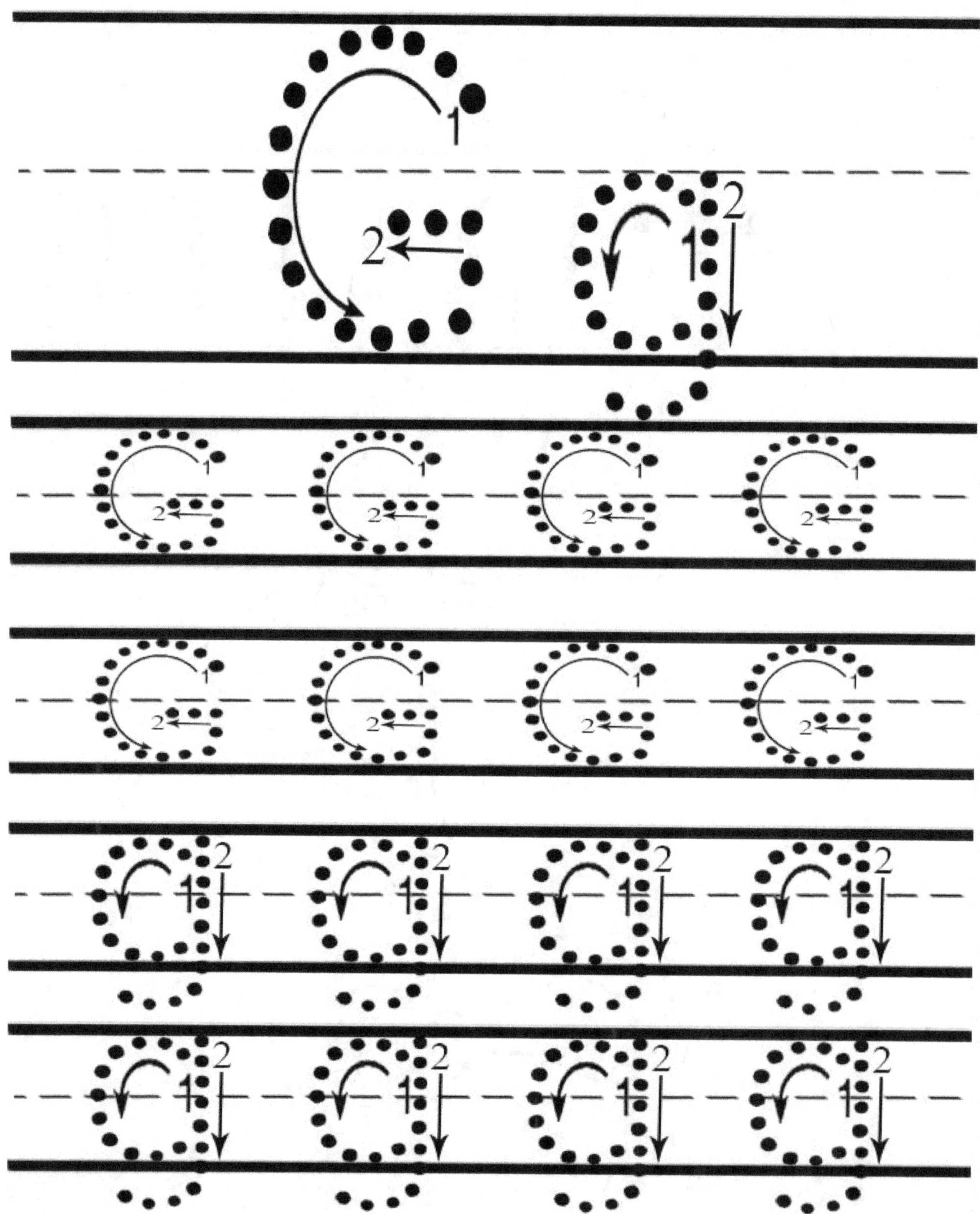

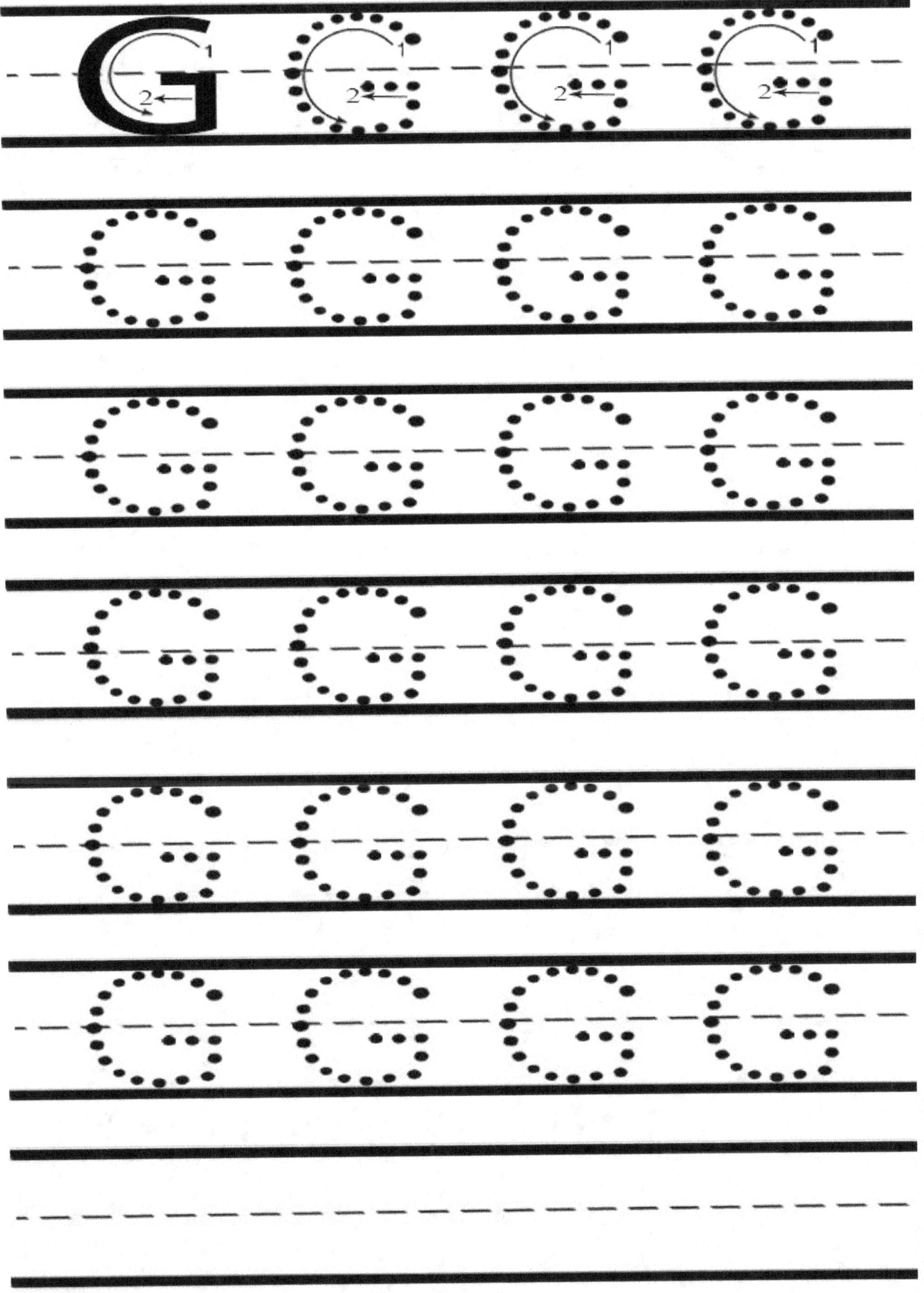

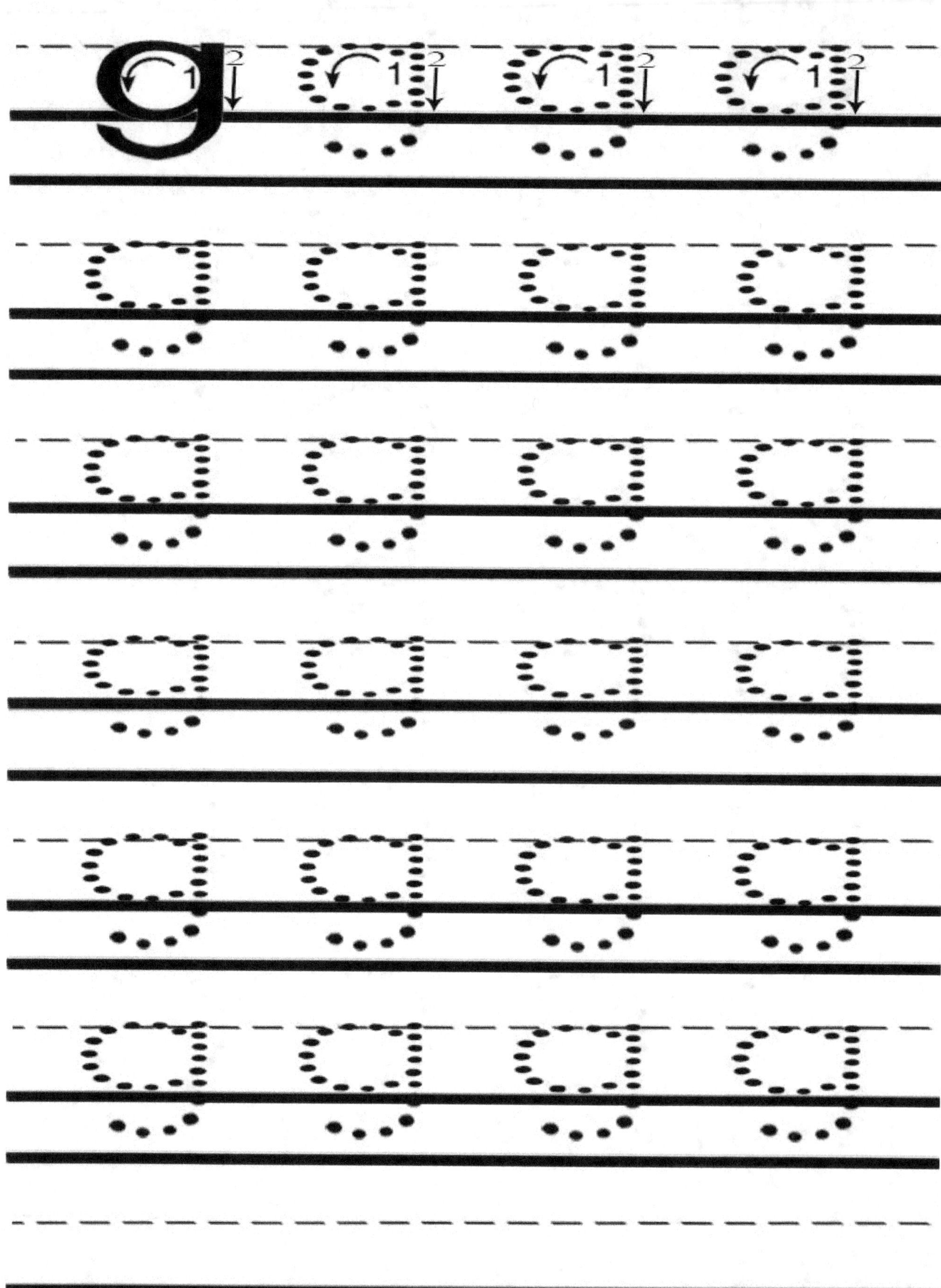

H is for

The Letter H

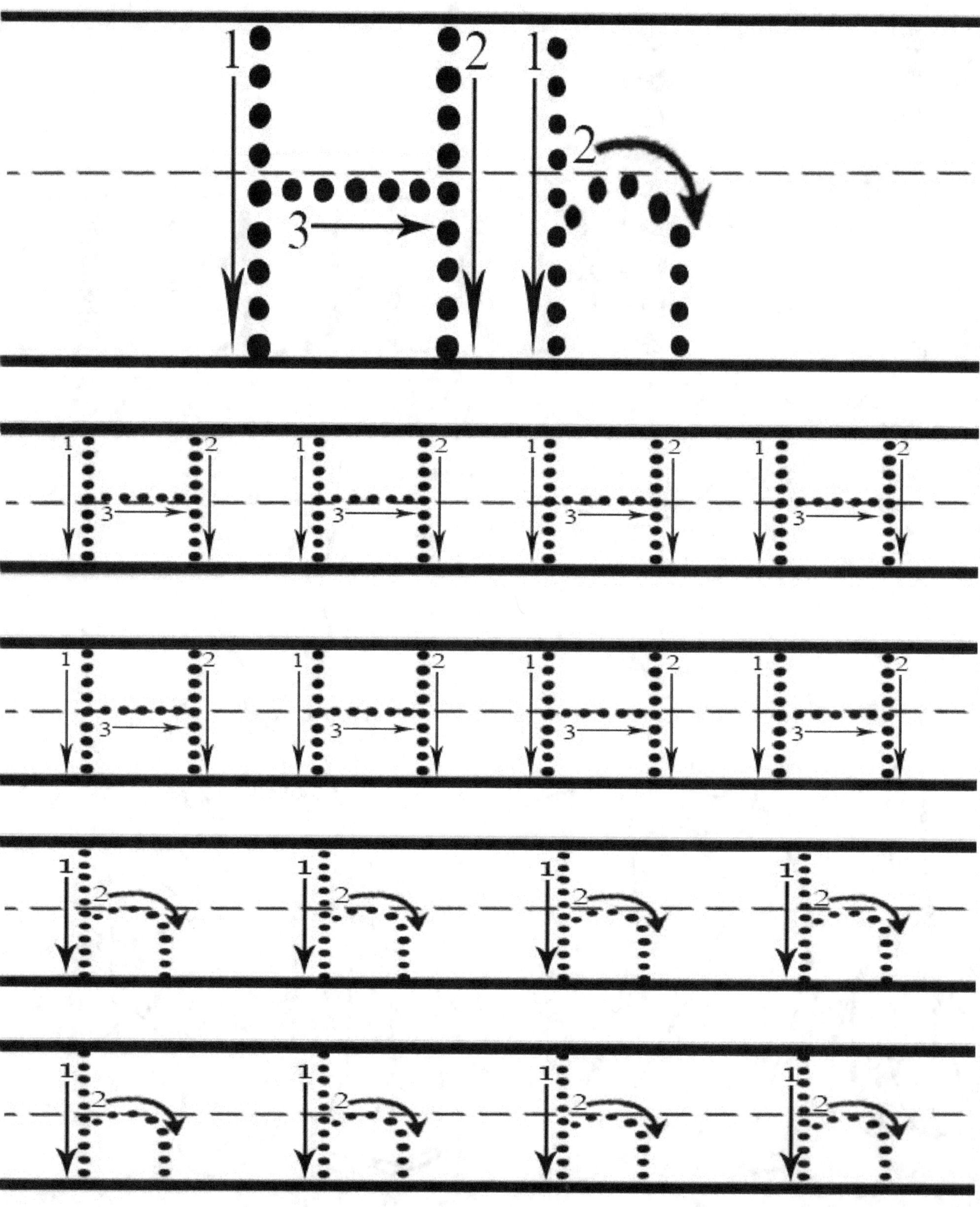

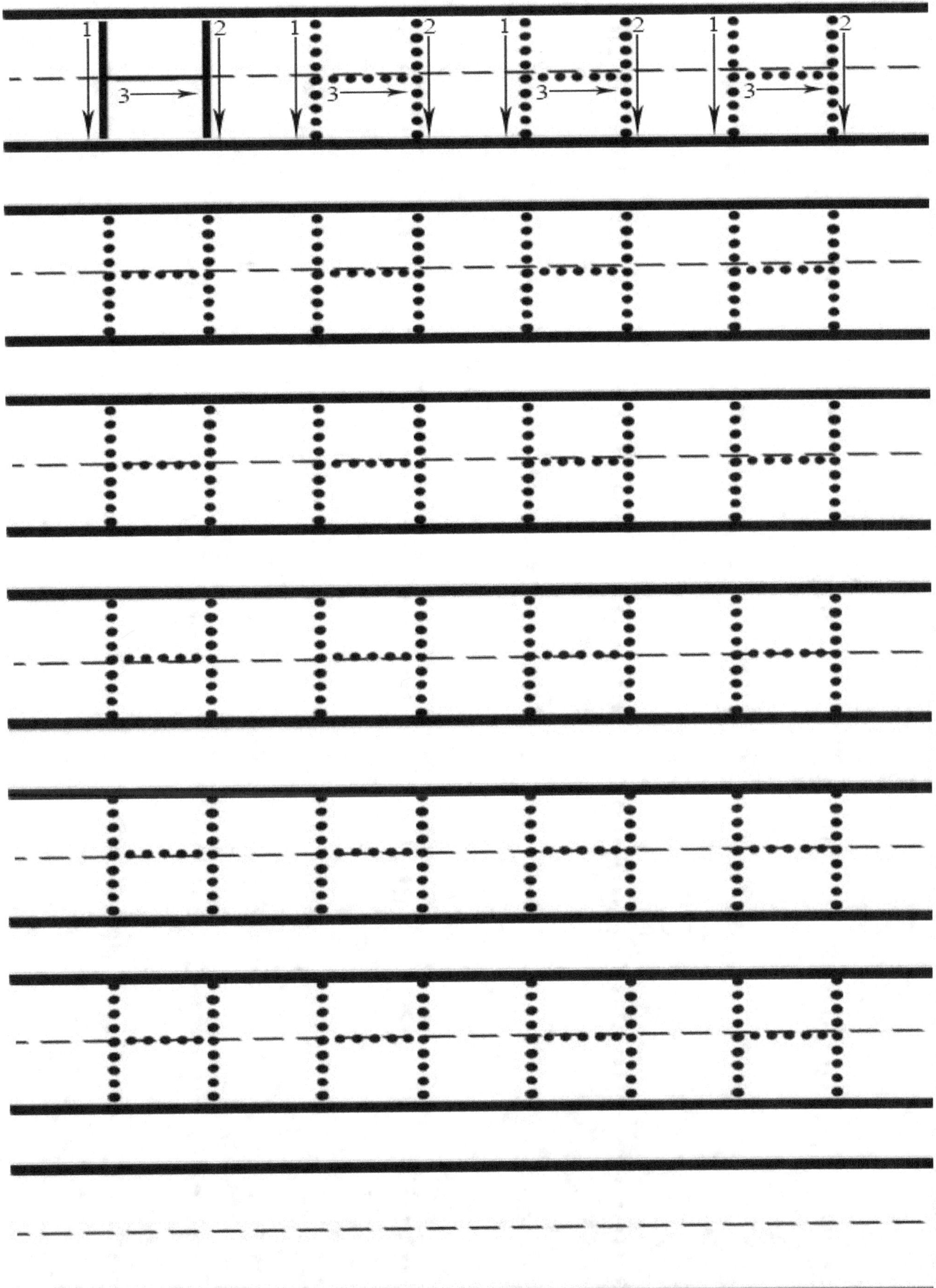

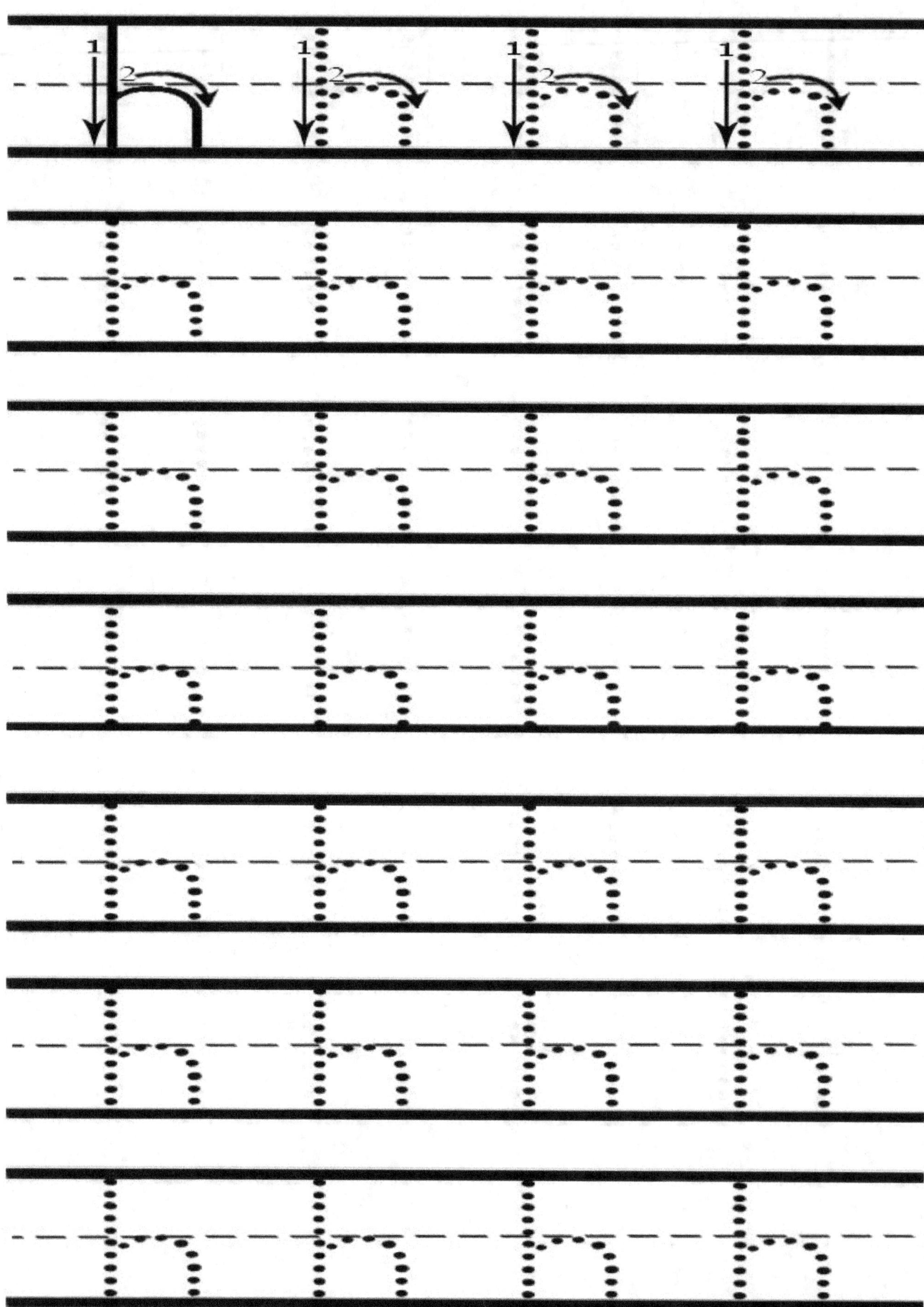

I is for

IGUANA

The Letter I

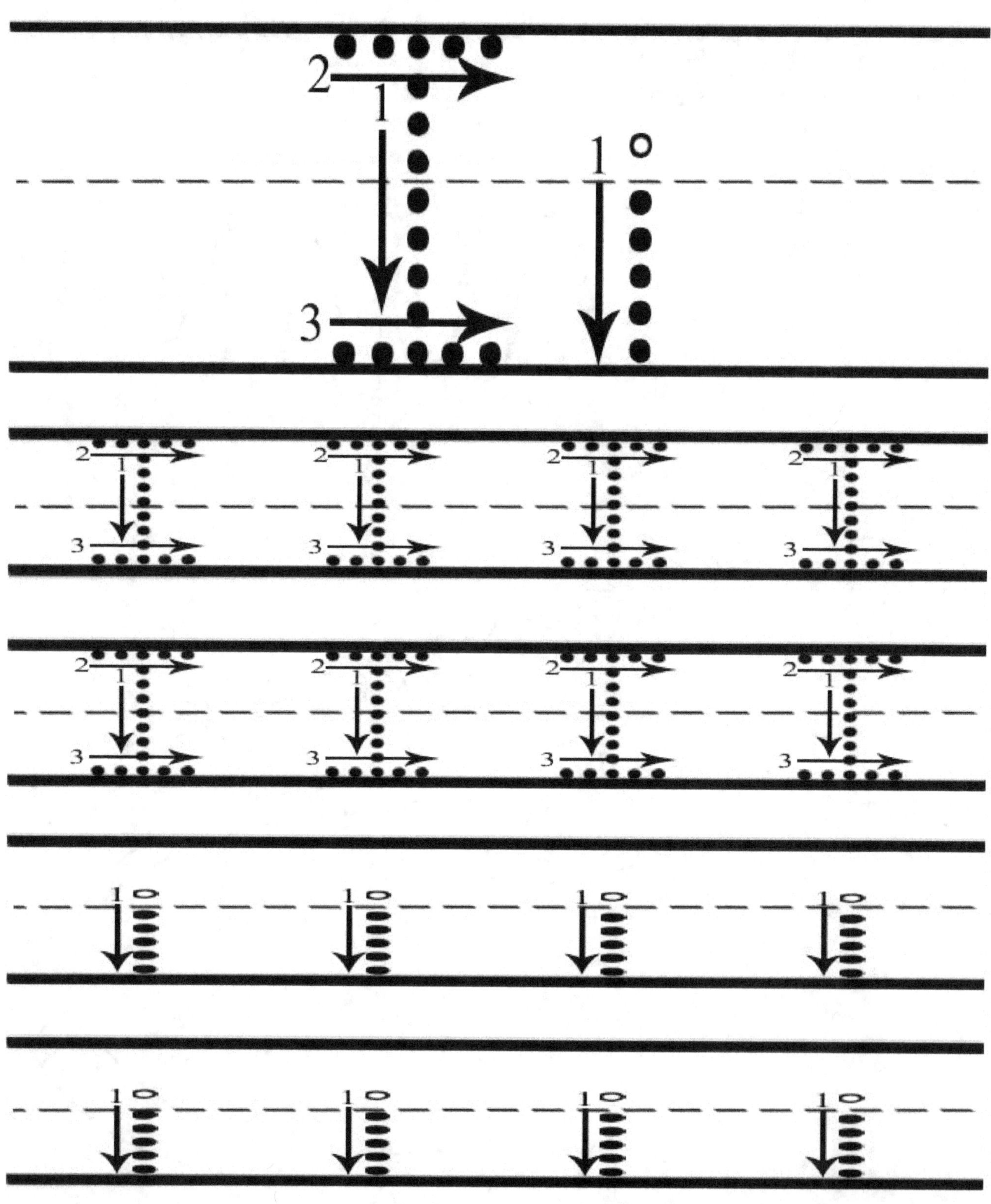

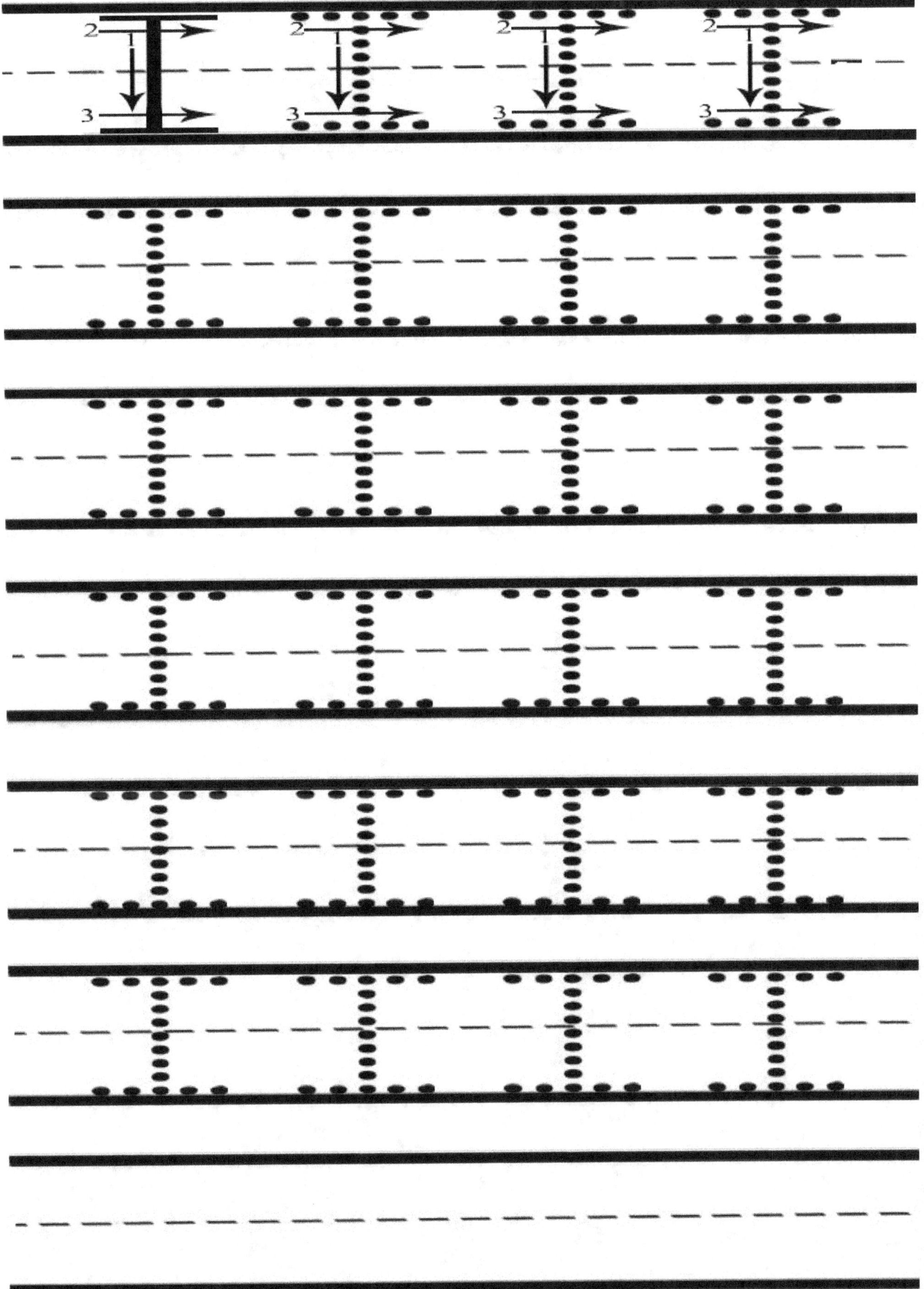

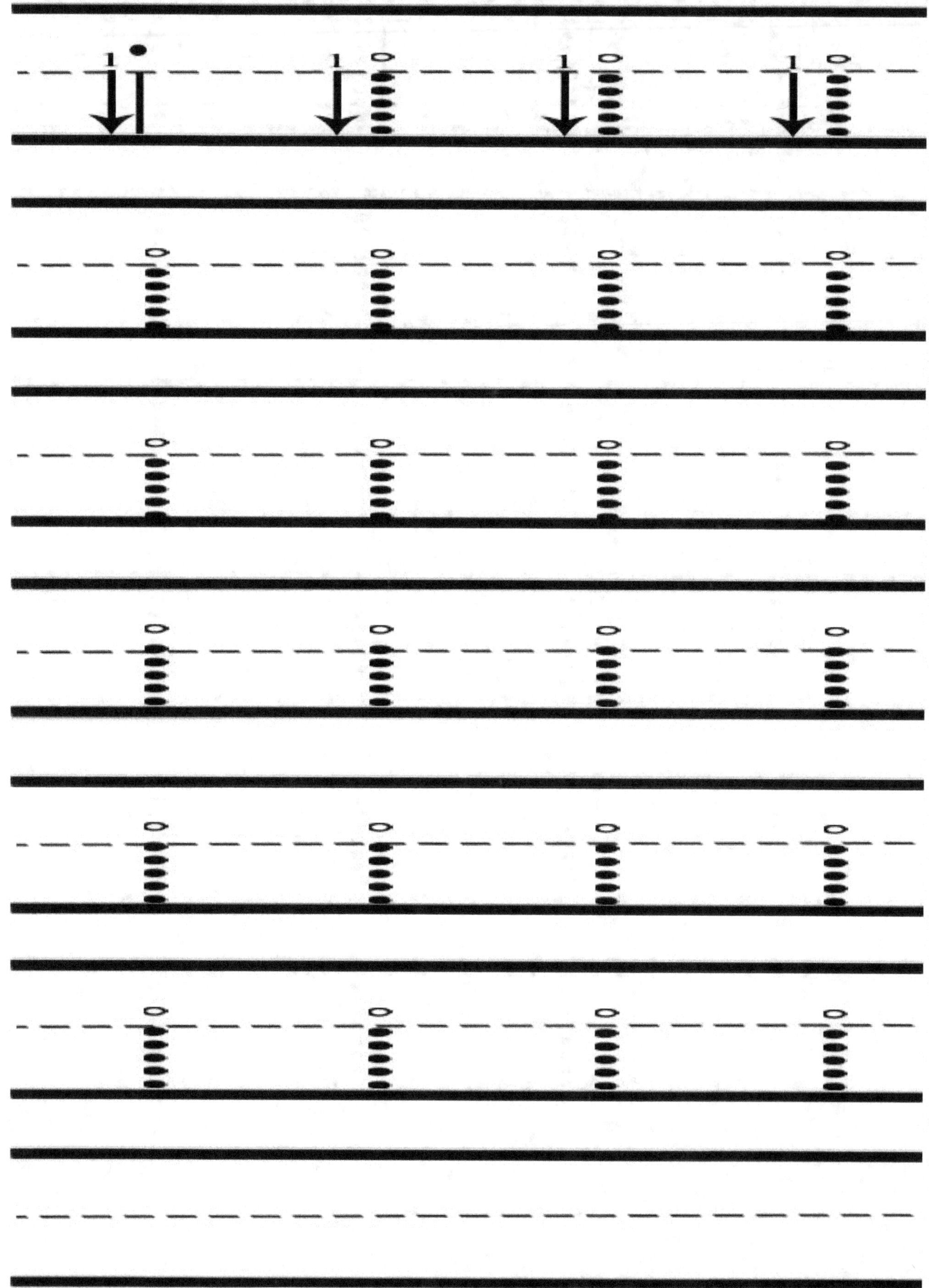

J is for

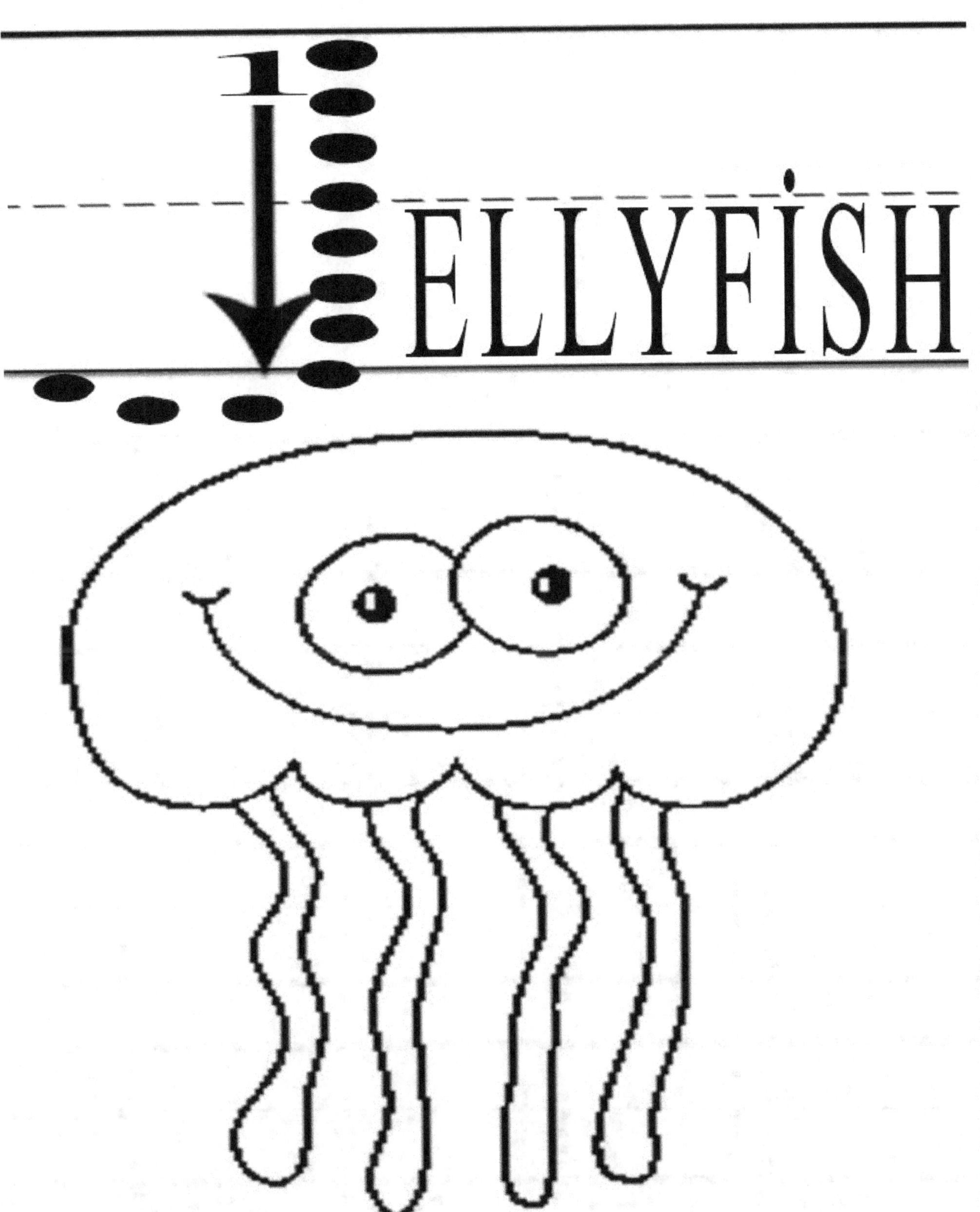

The Letter J

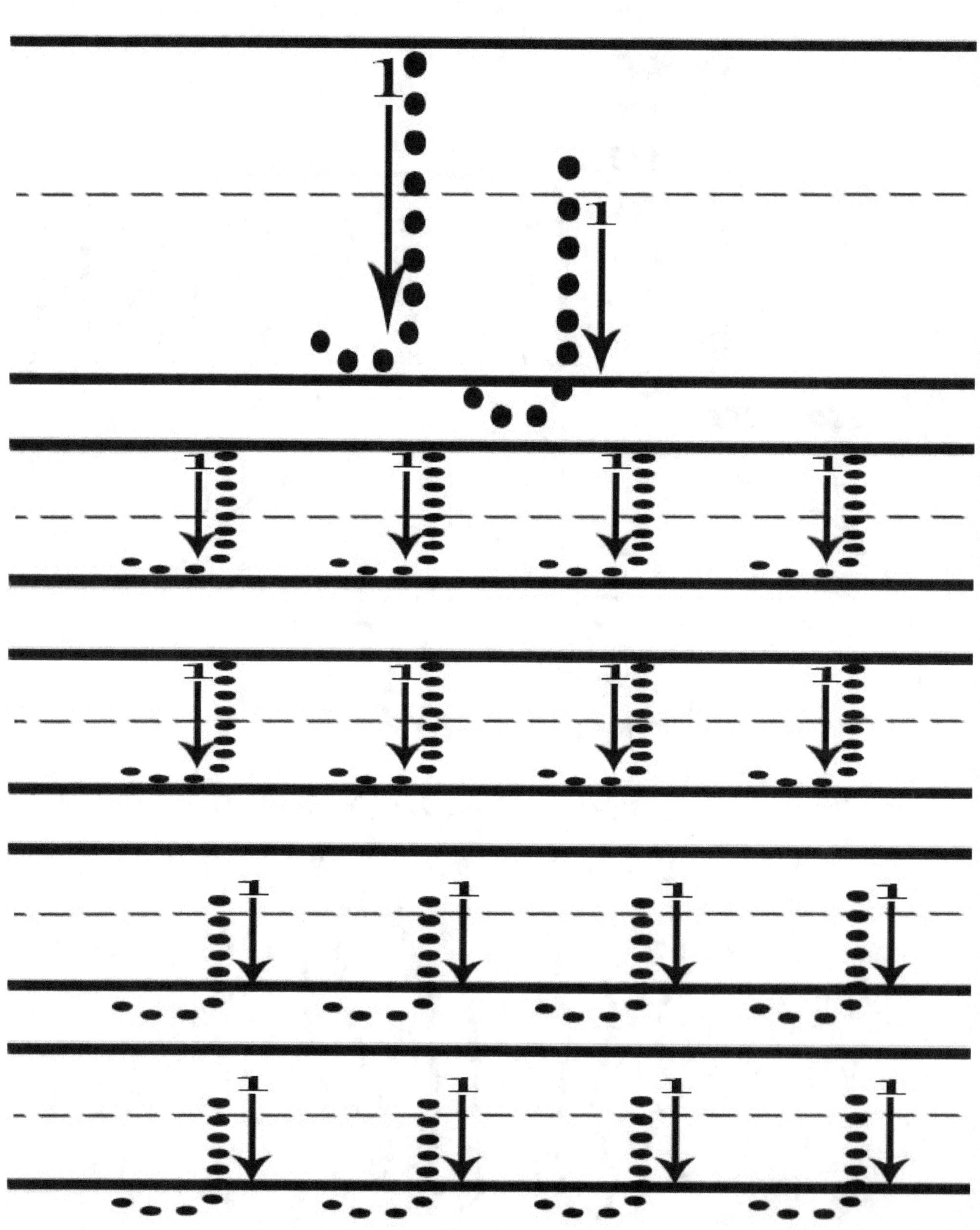

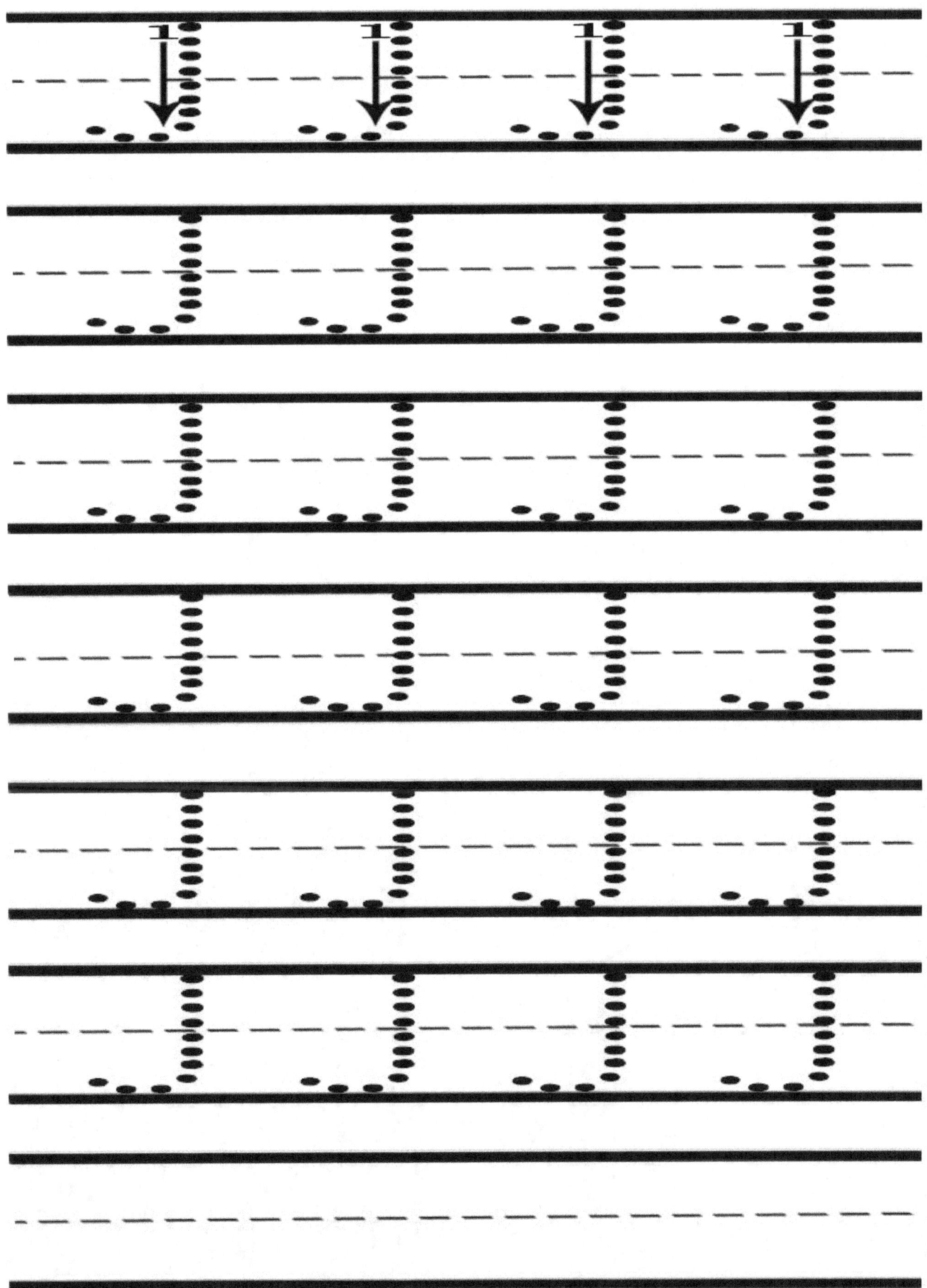

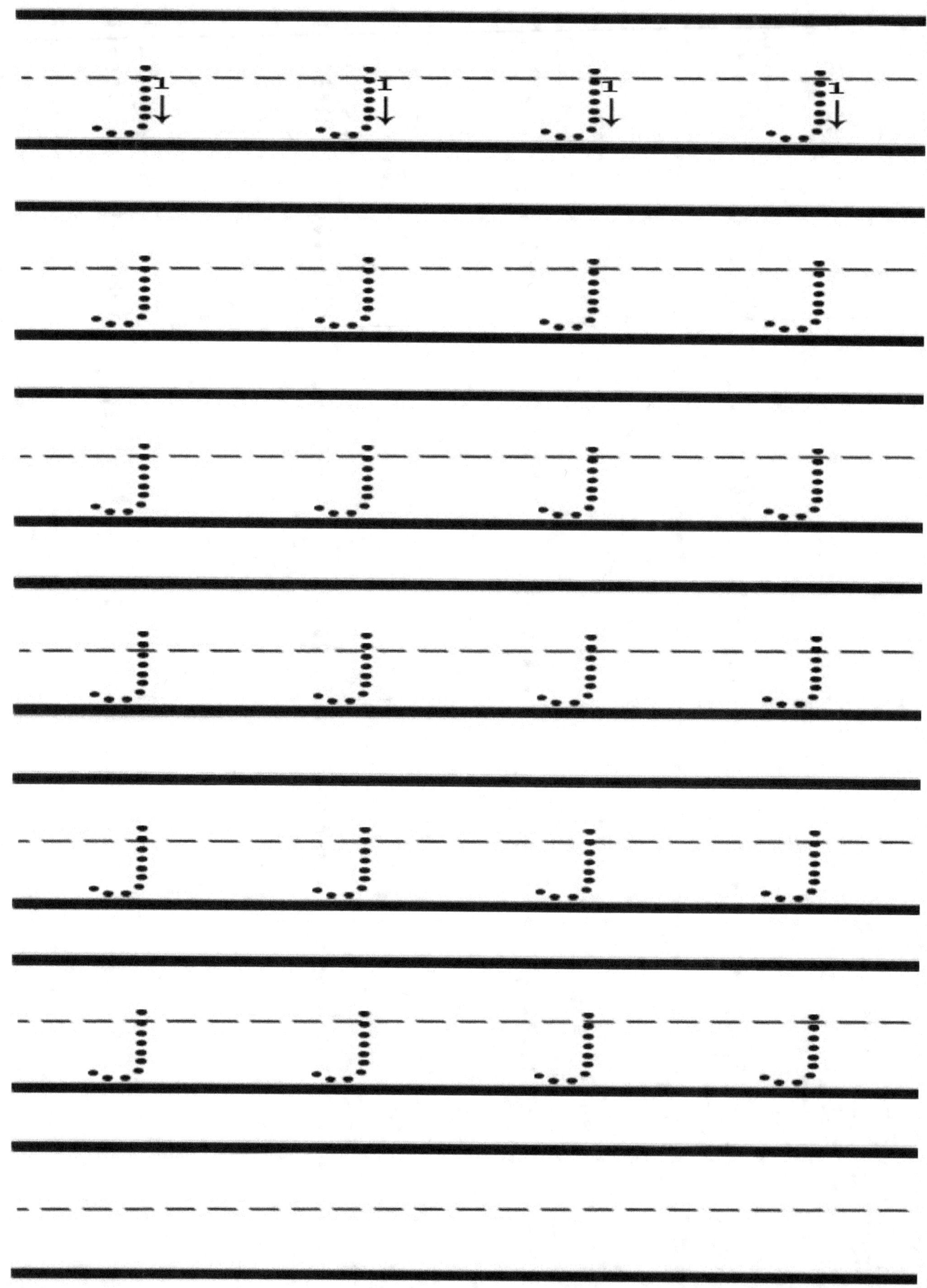

K is for

The Letter K

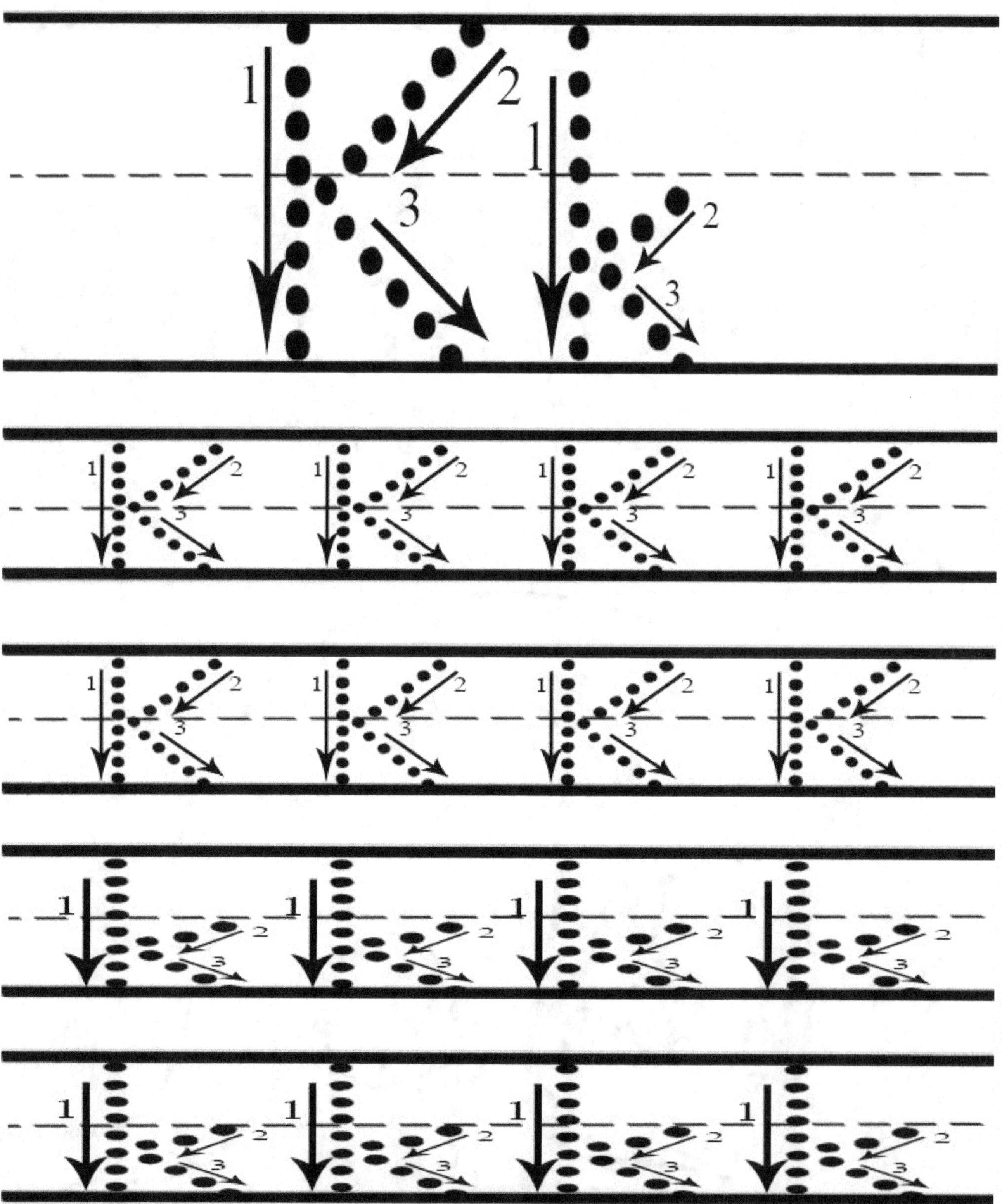

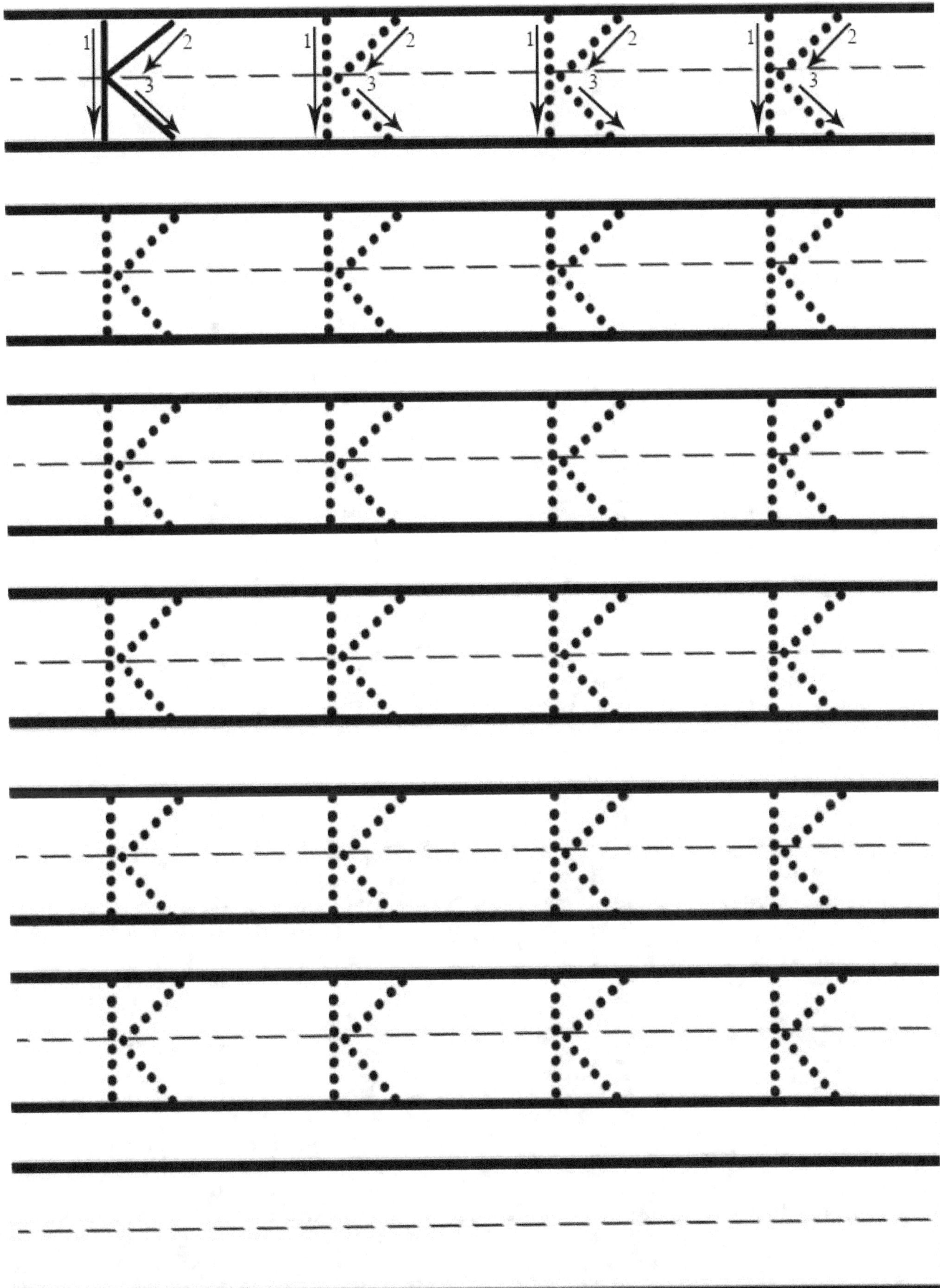

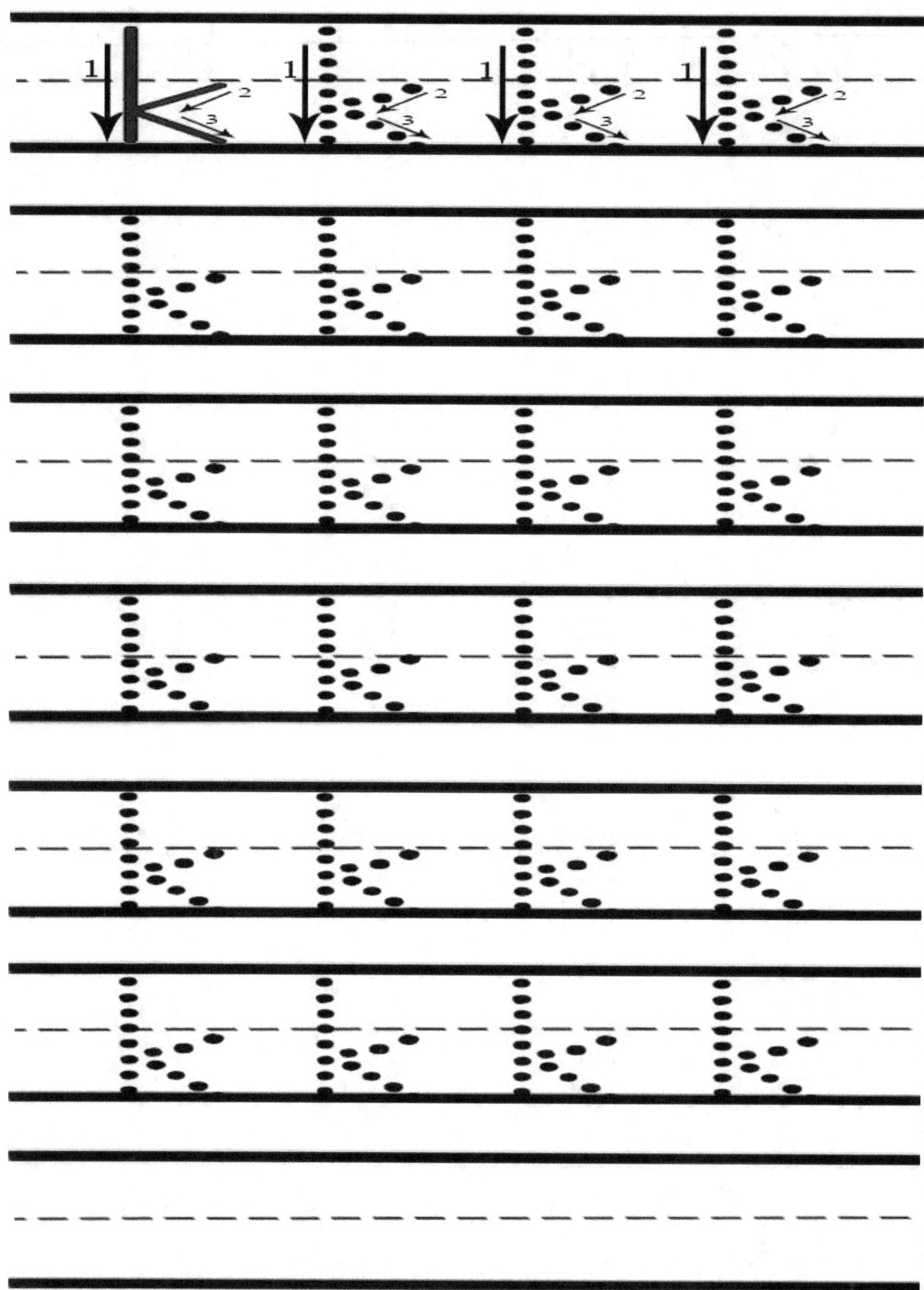

L is for

The Letter L

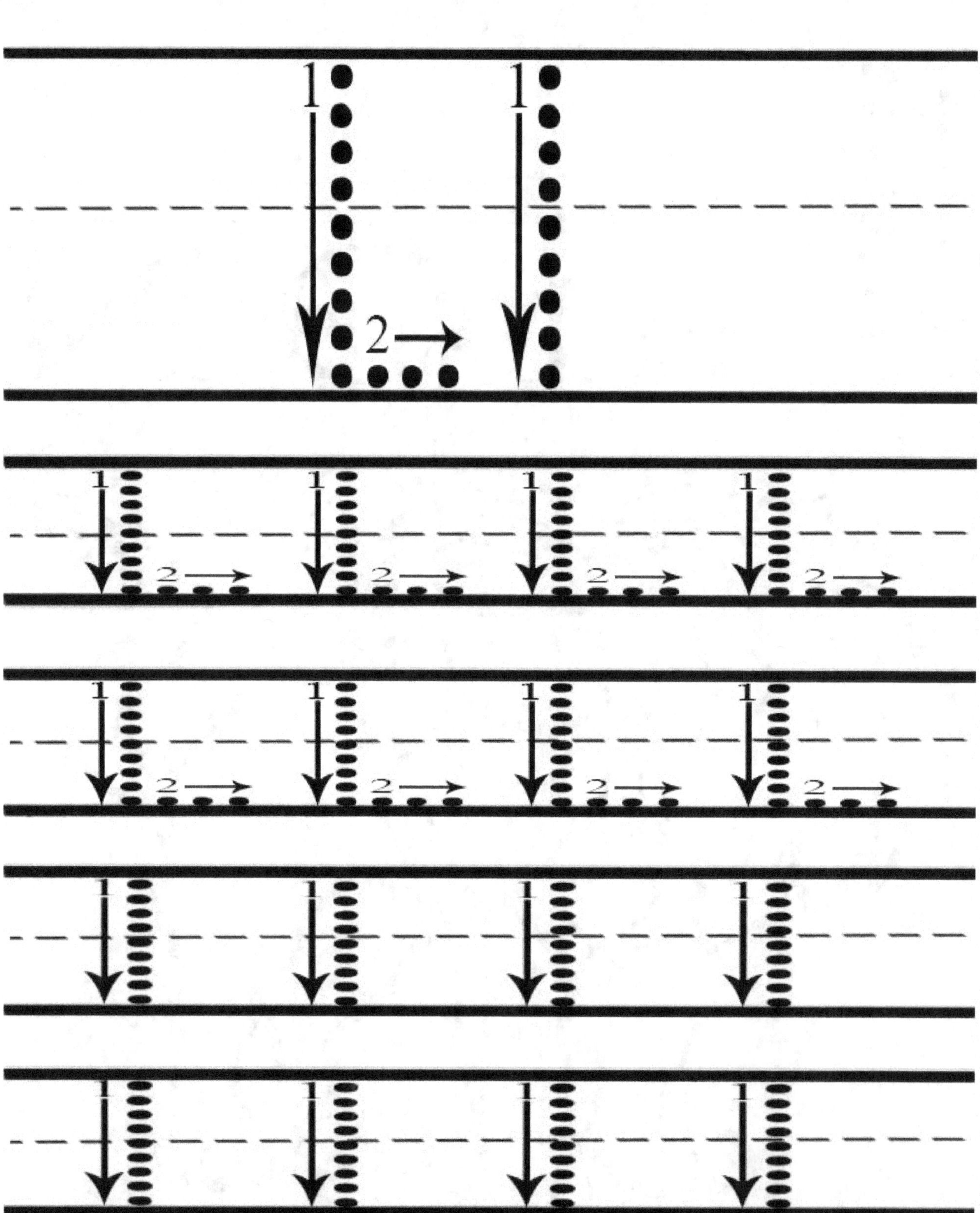

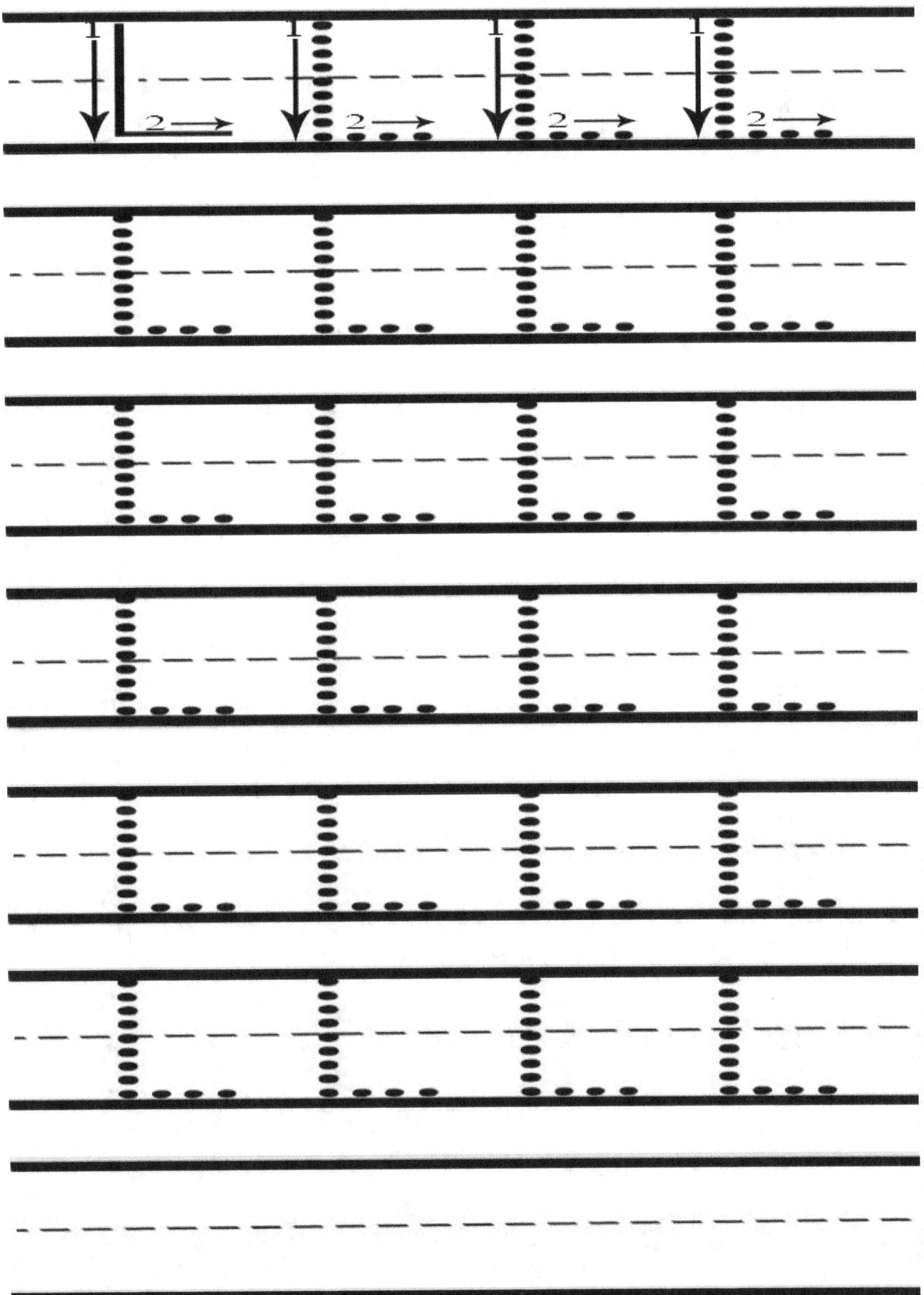

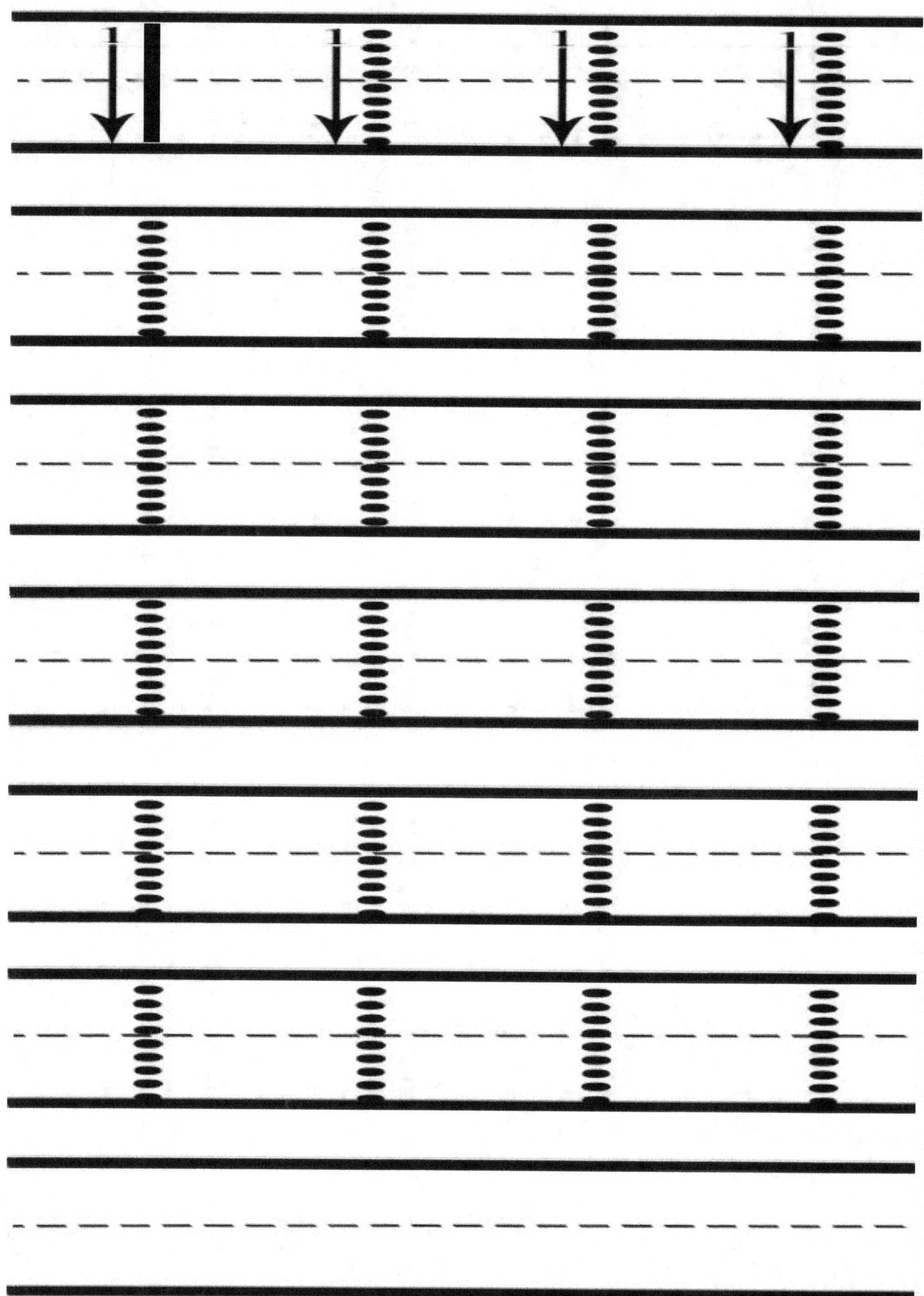

M is for

The Letter M

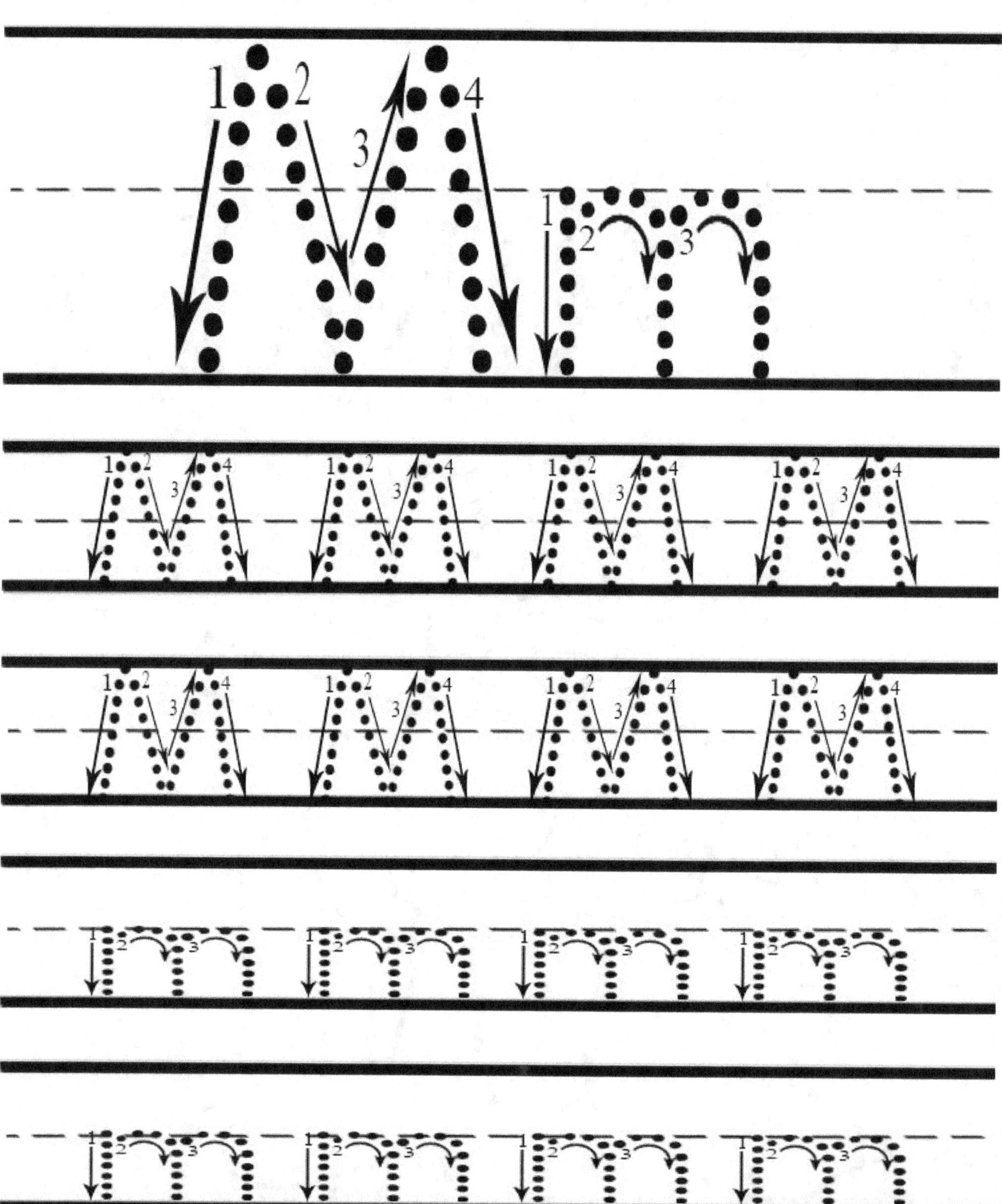

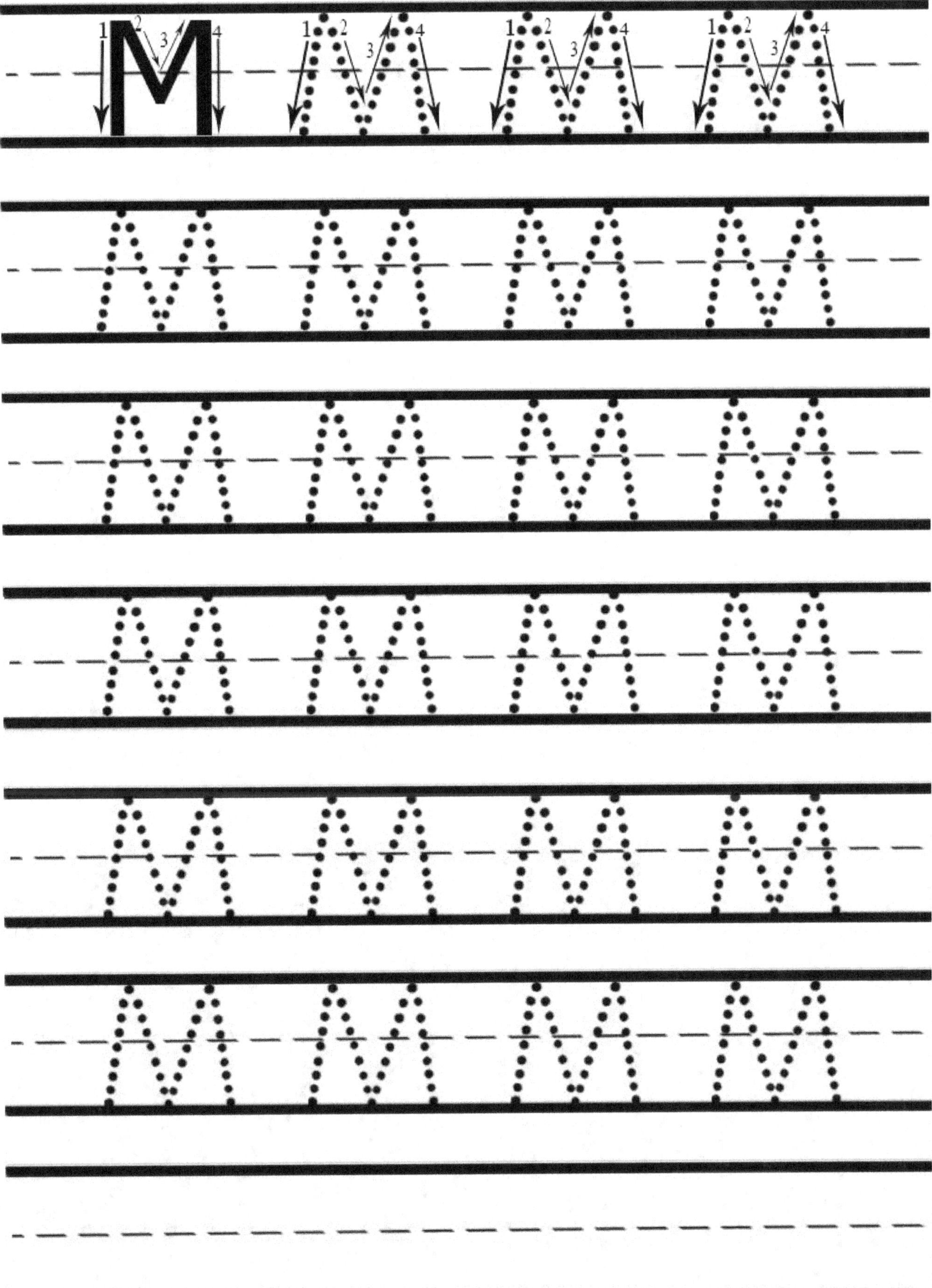

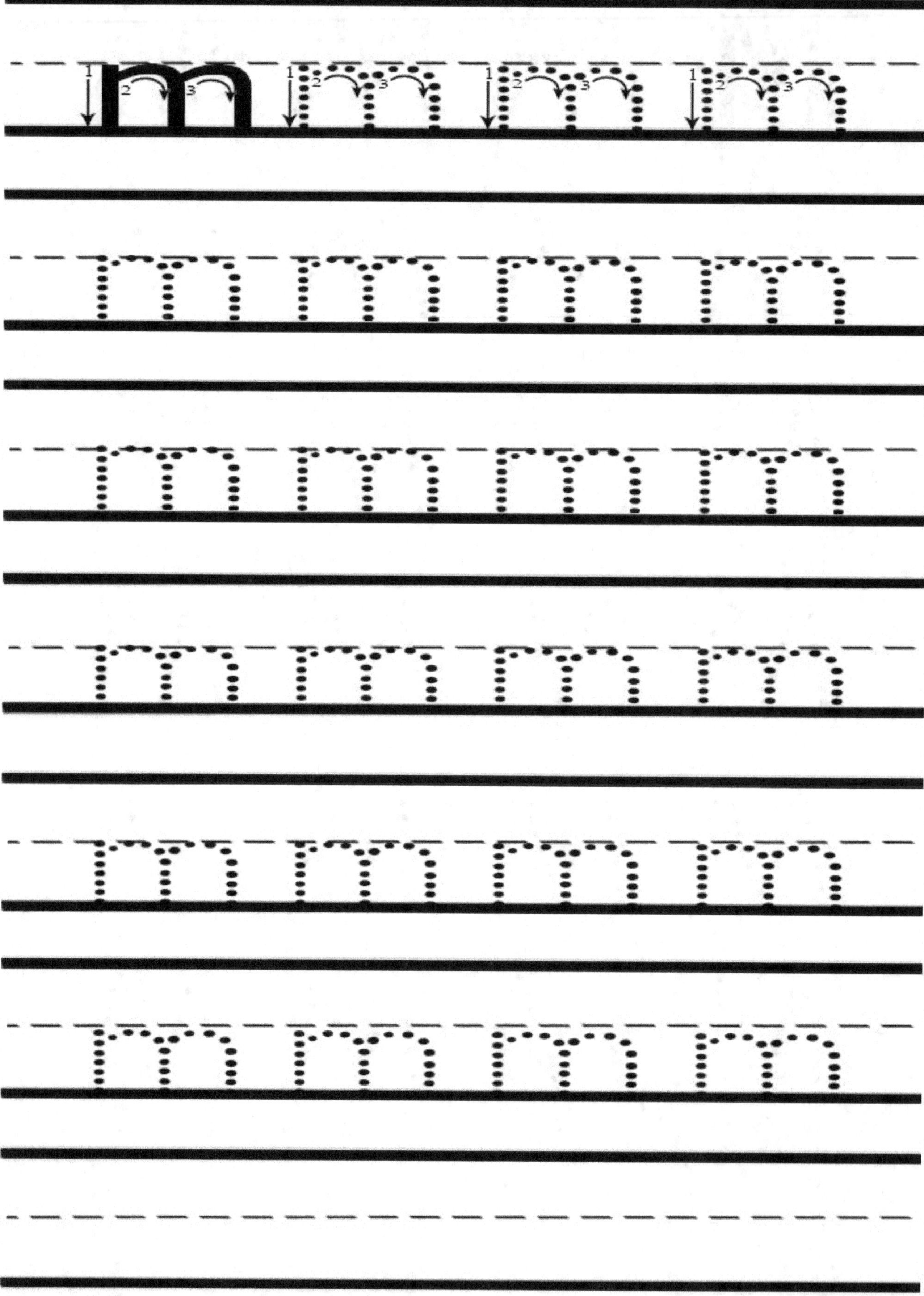

N is for

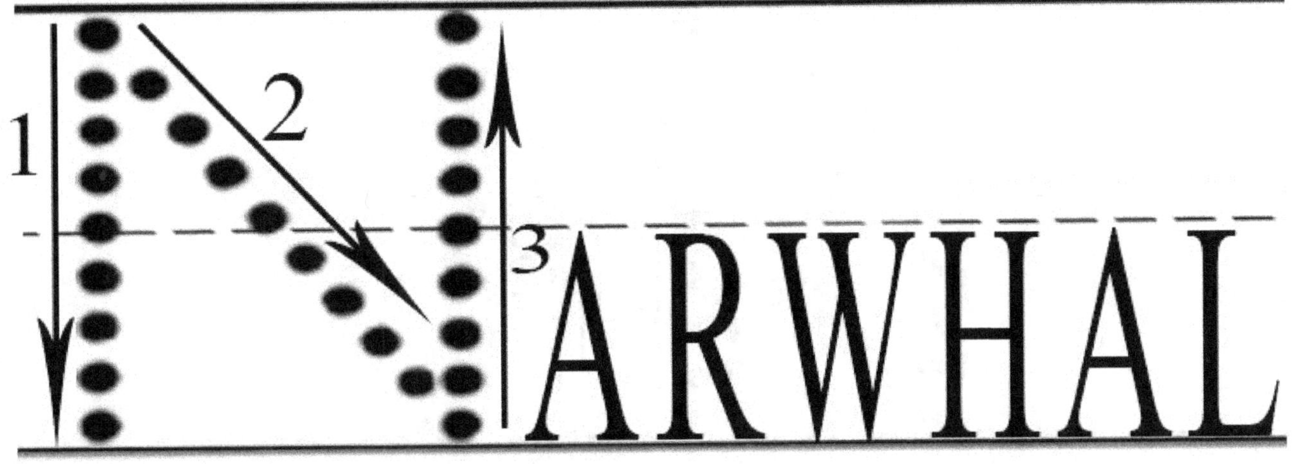

The Letter N

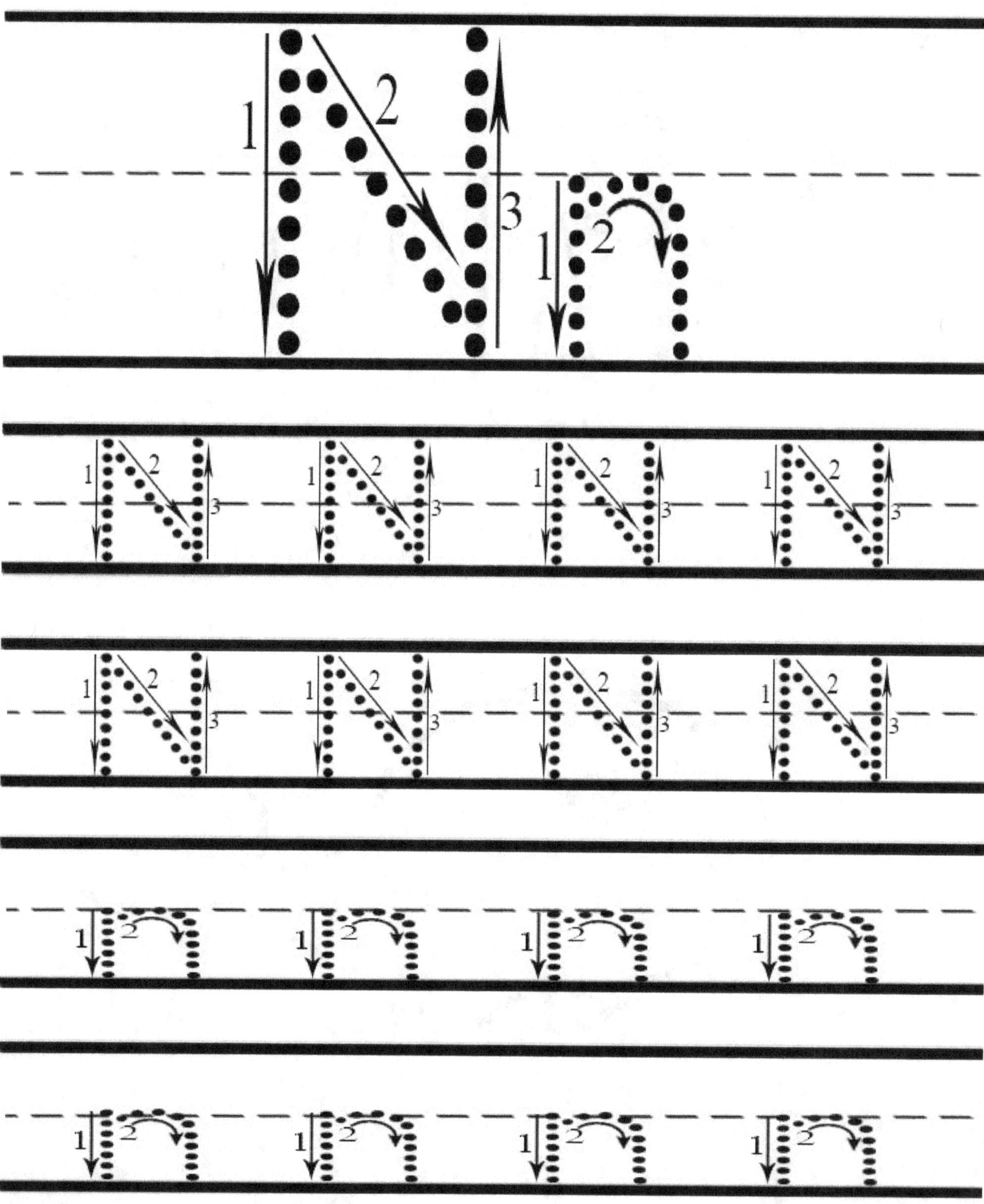

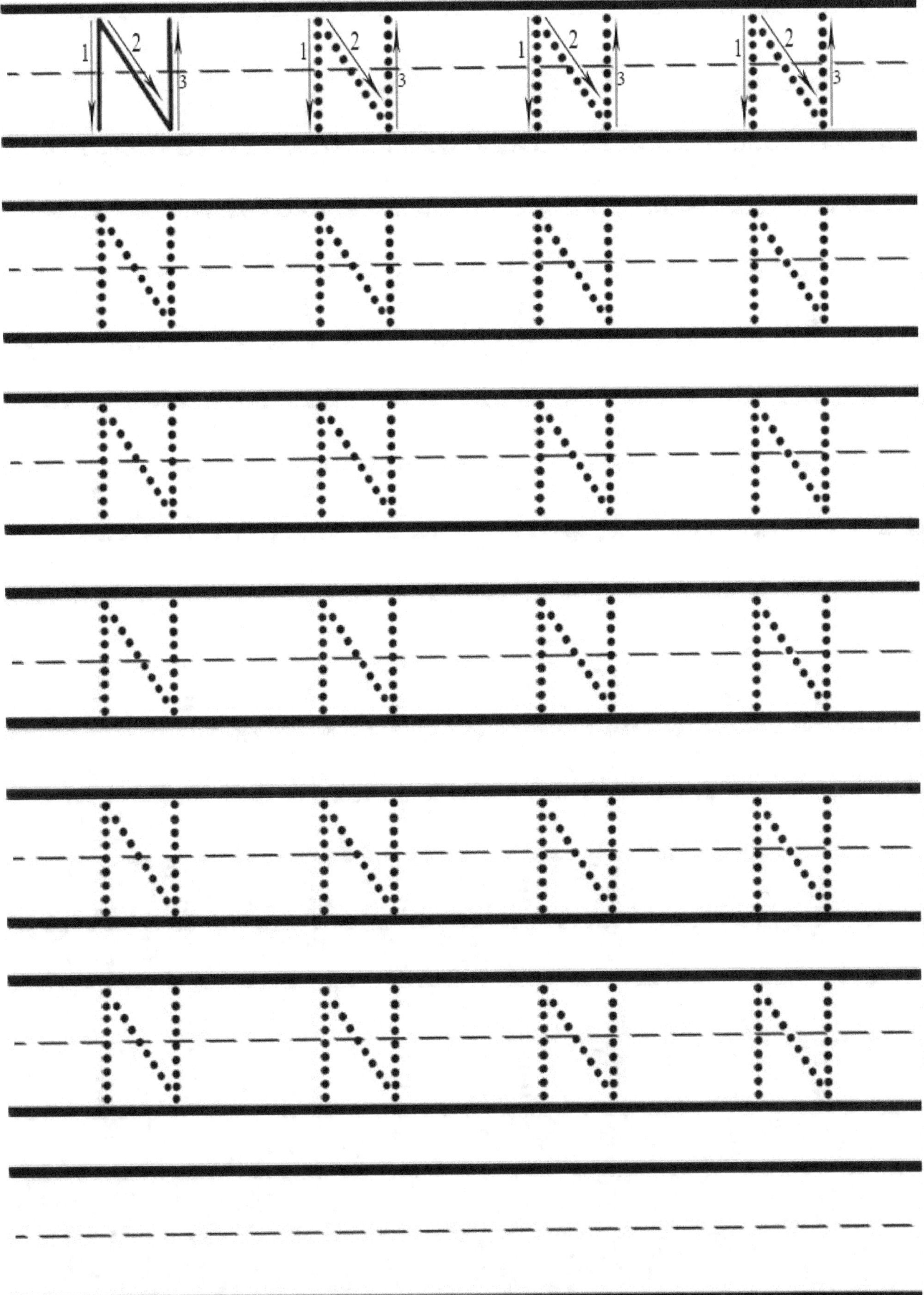

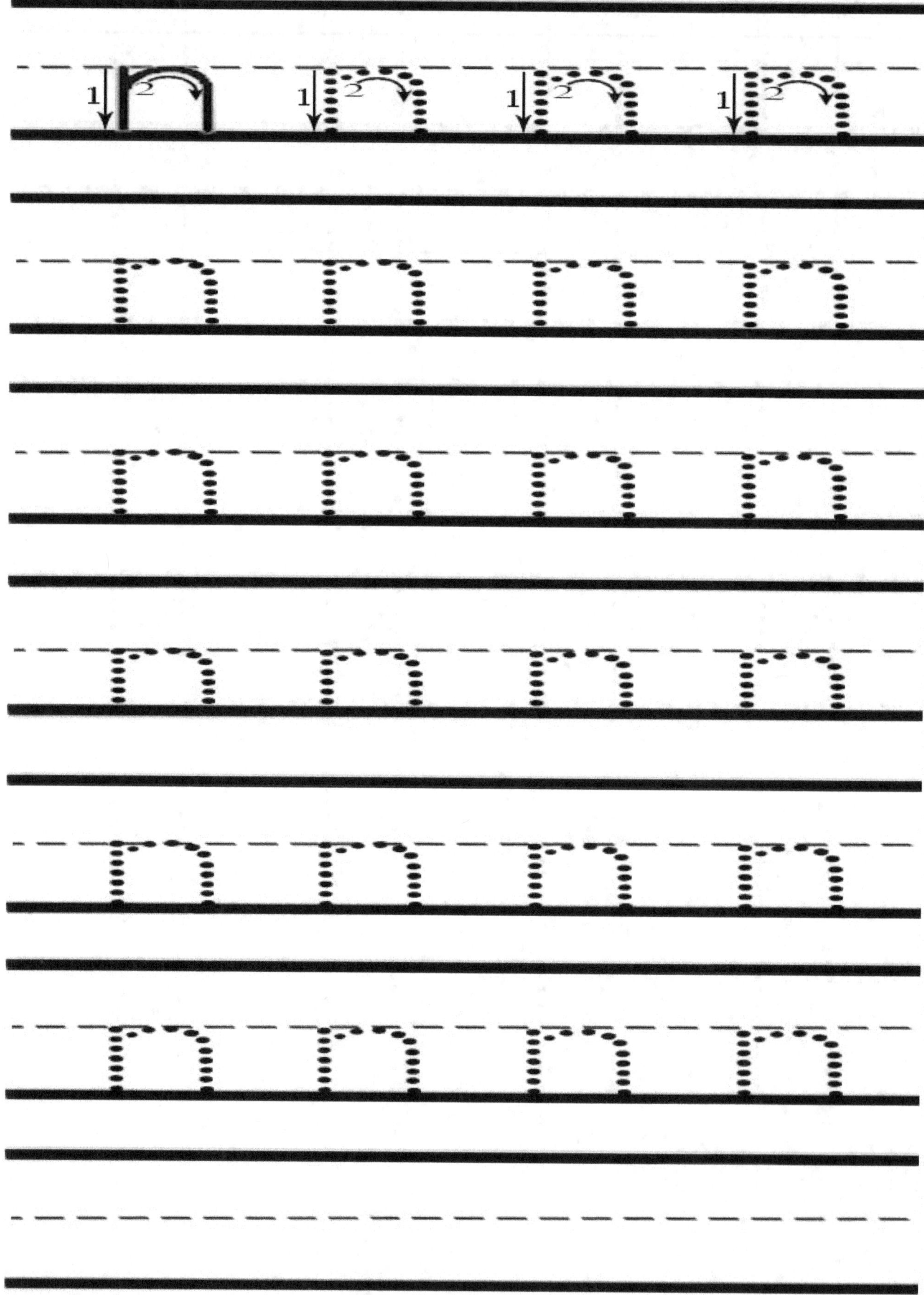

O is for

The Letter O

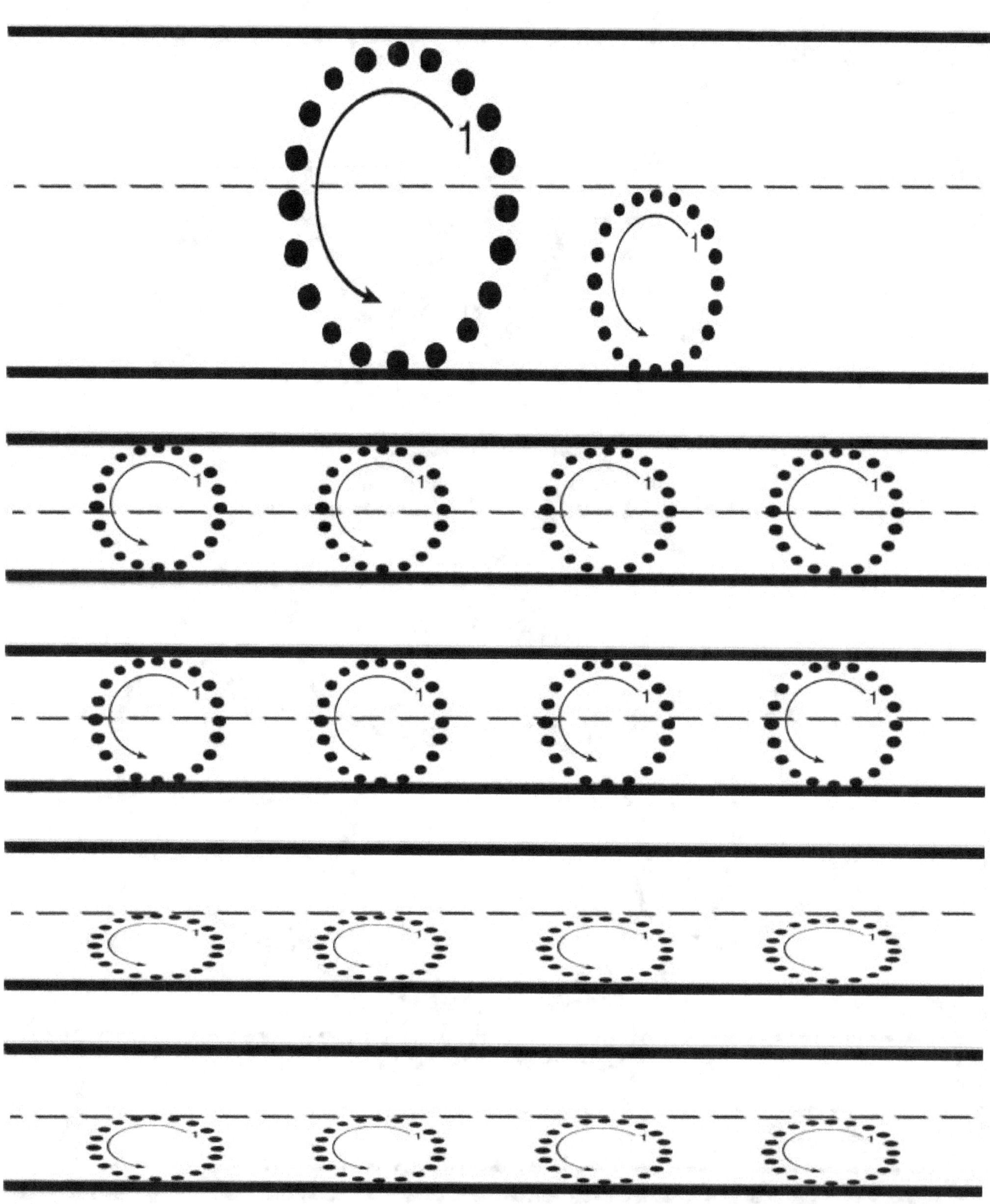

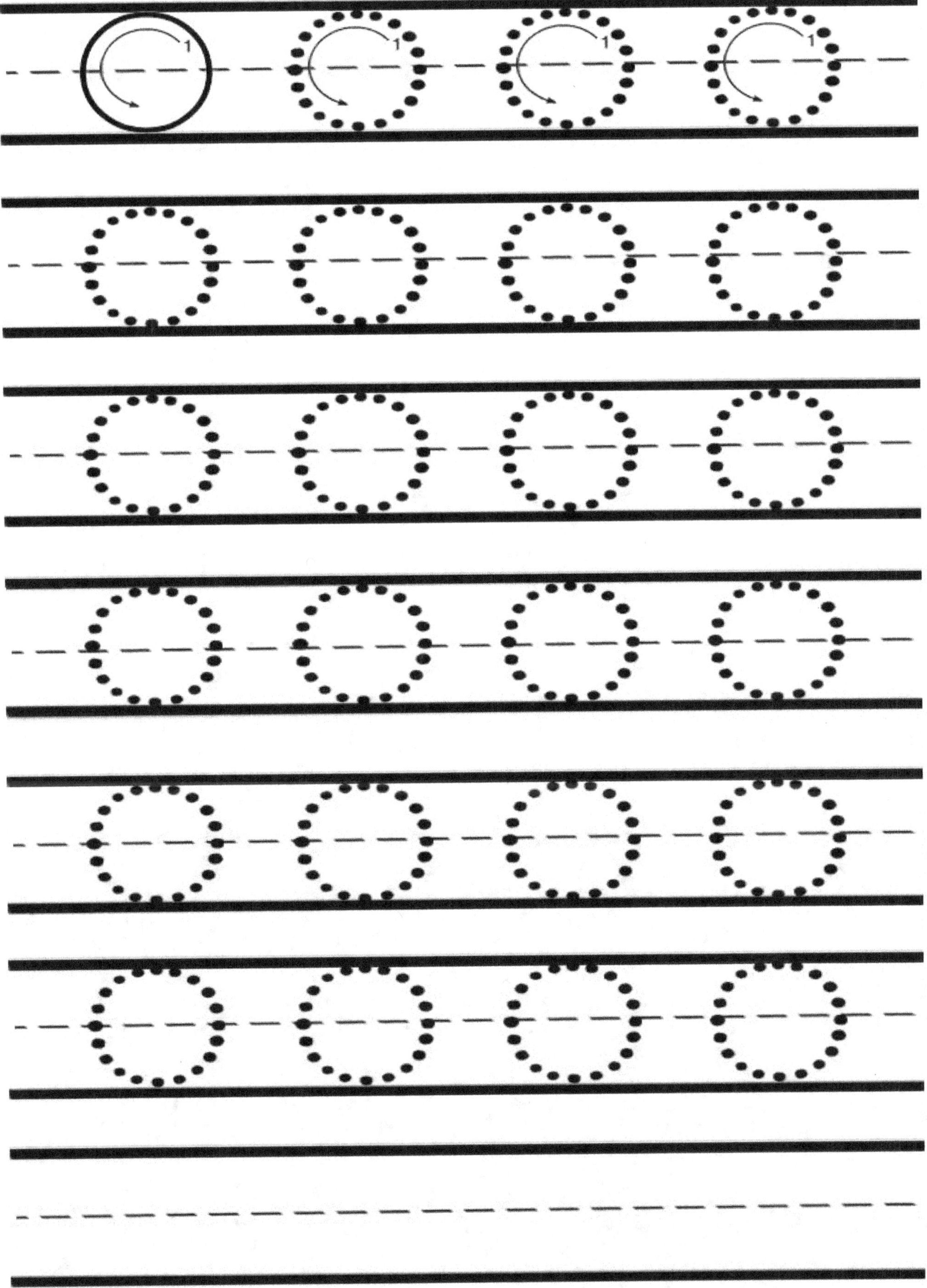

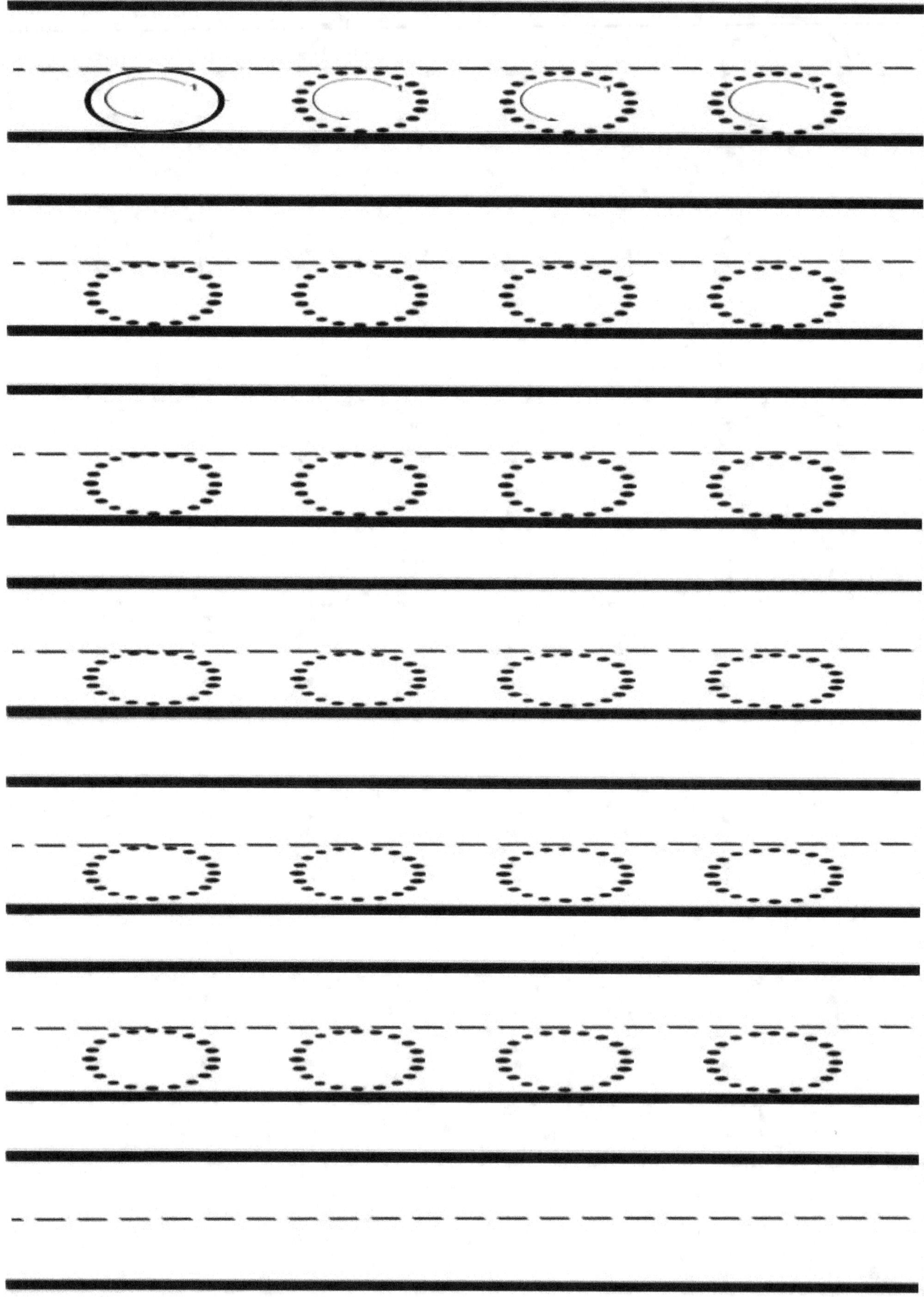

P is for

The Letter P

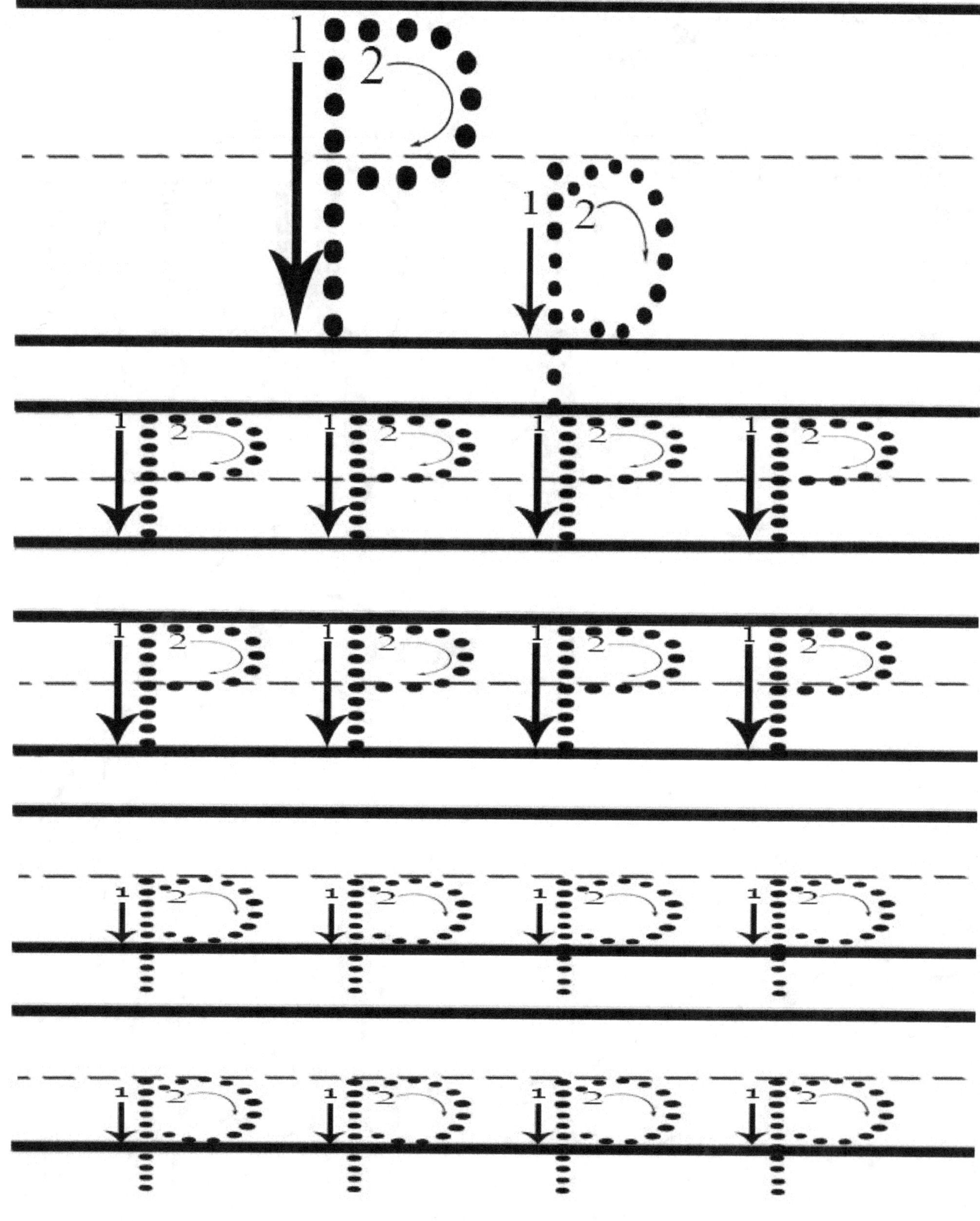

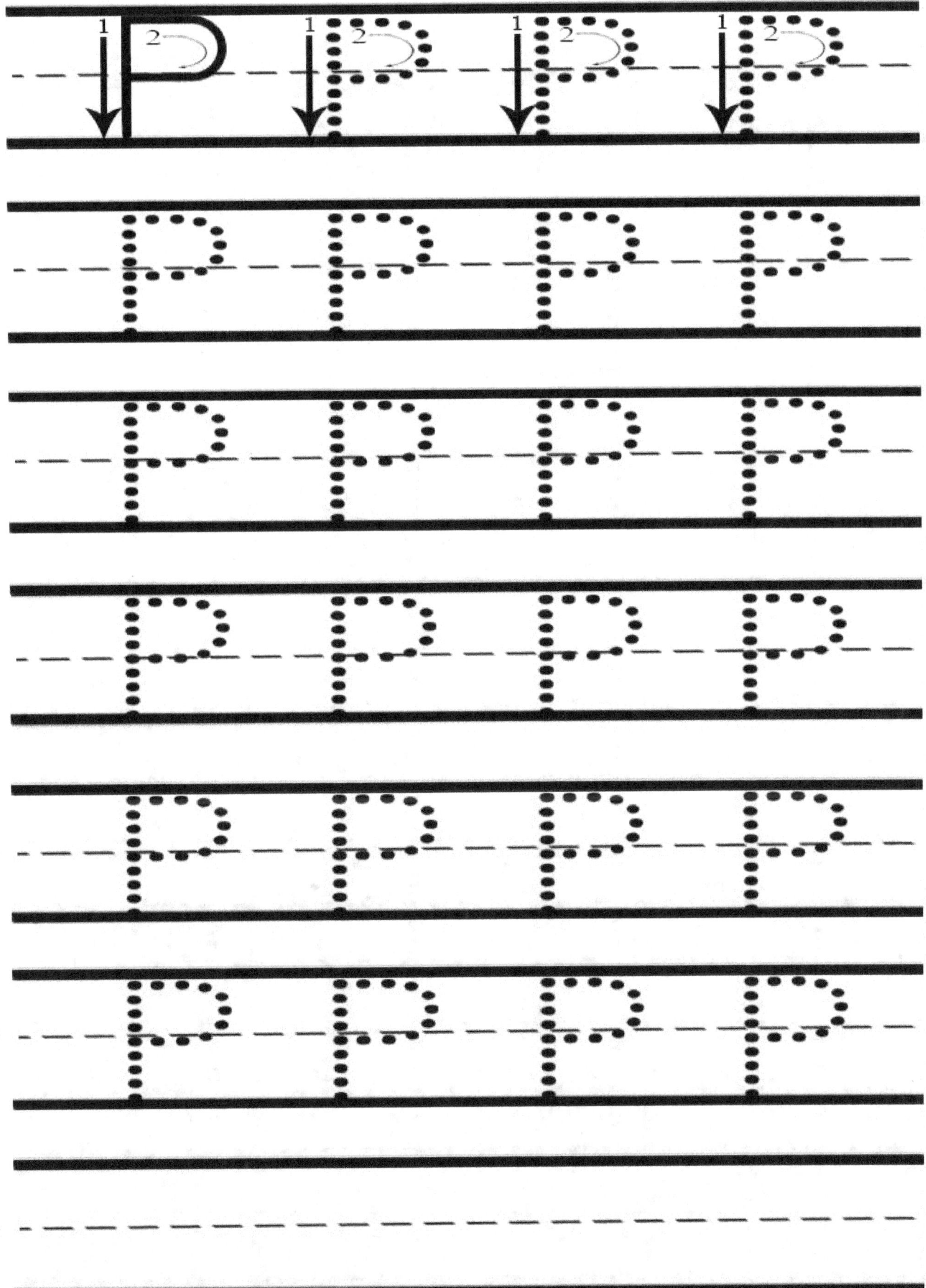

1 2

p p p p

p p p p

p p p p

p p p p

p p p p

p p p p

Q is for

The Letter Q

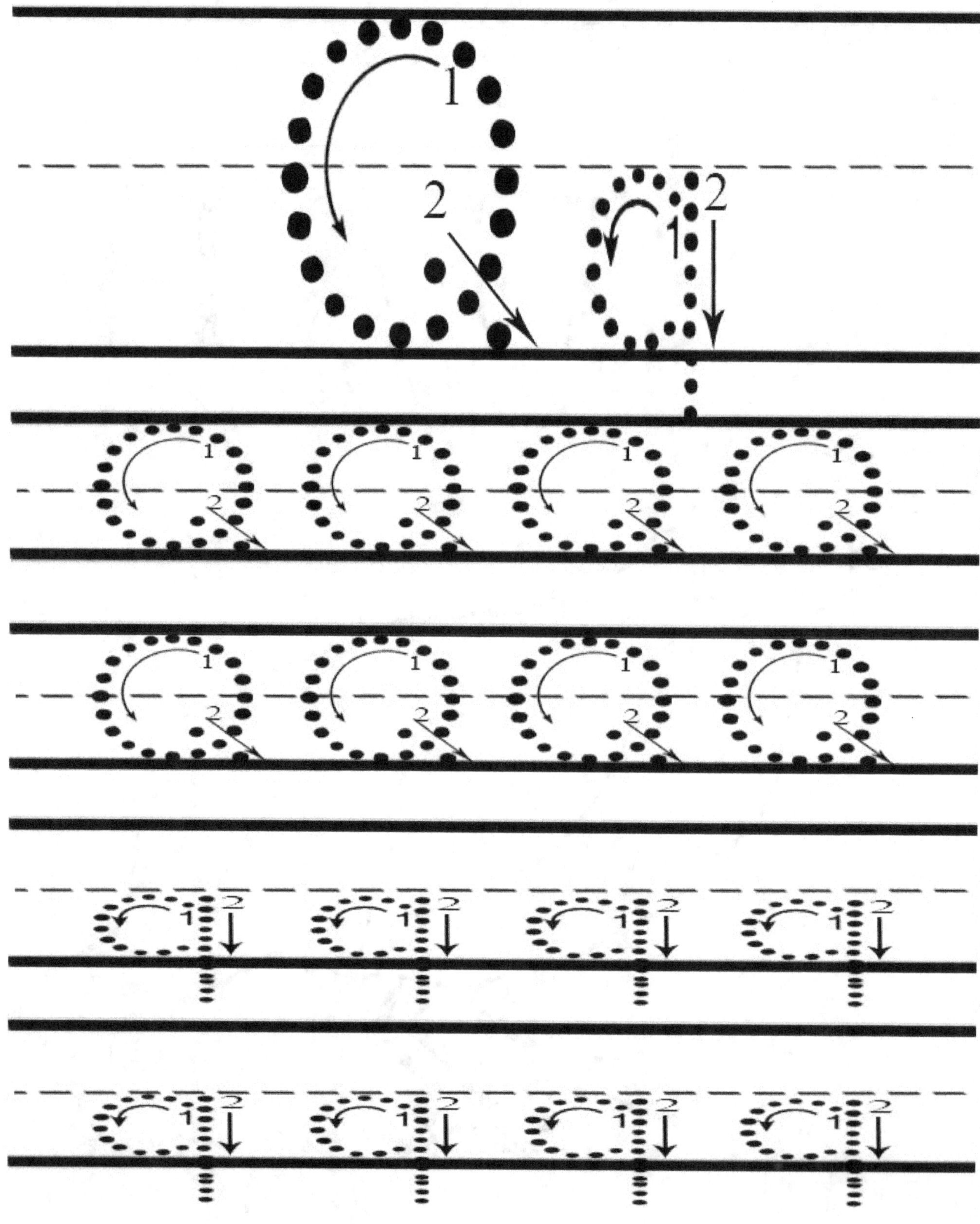

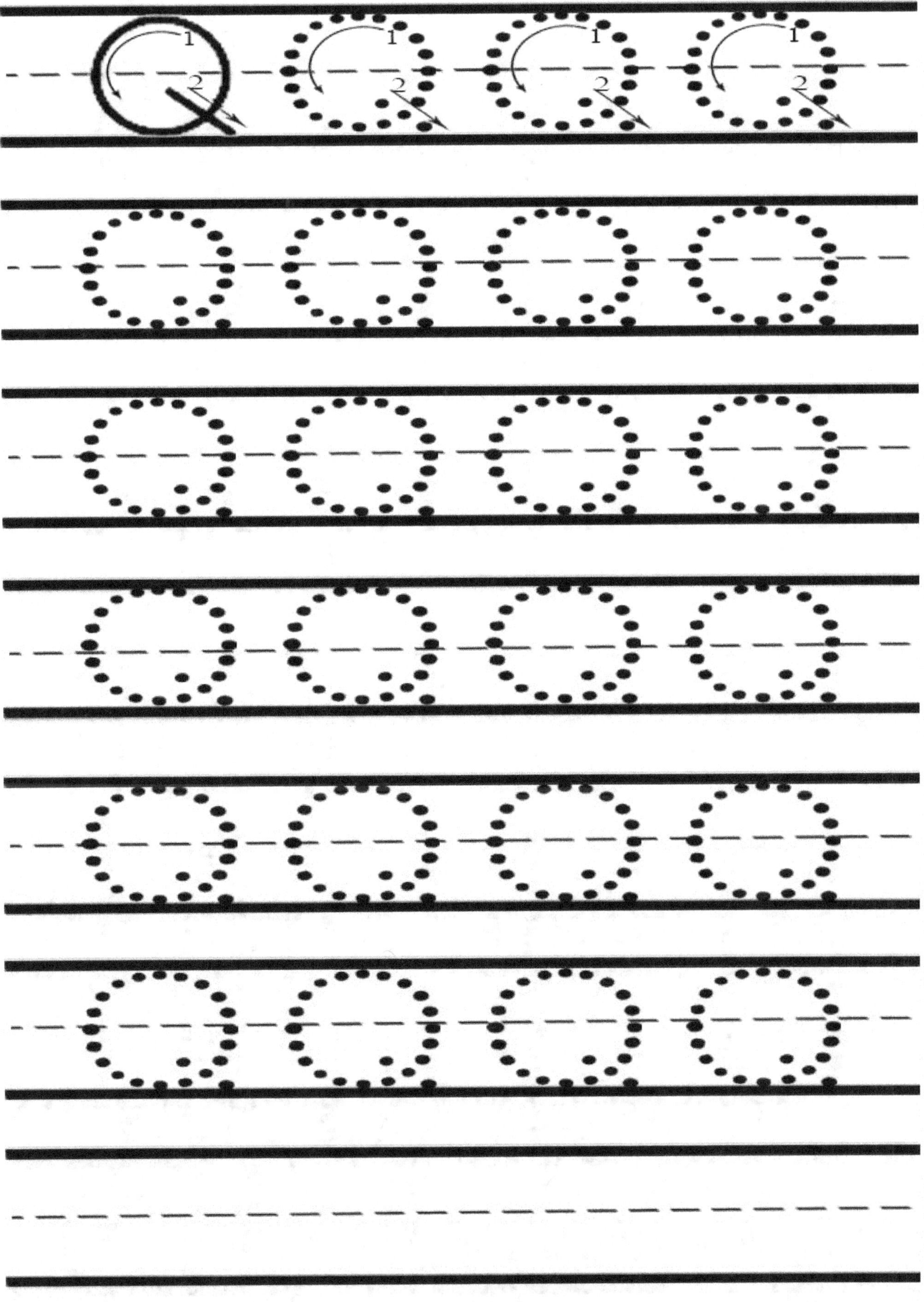

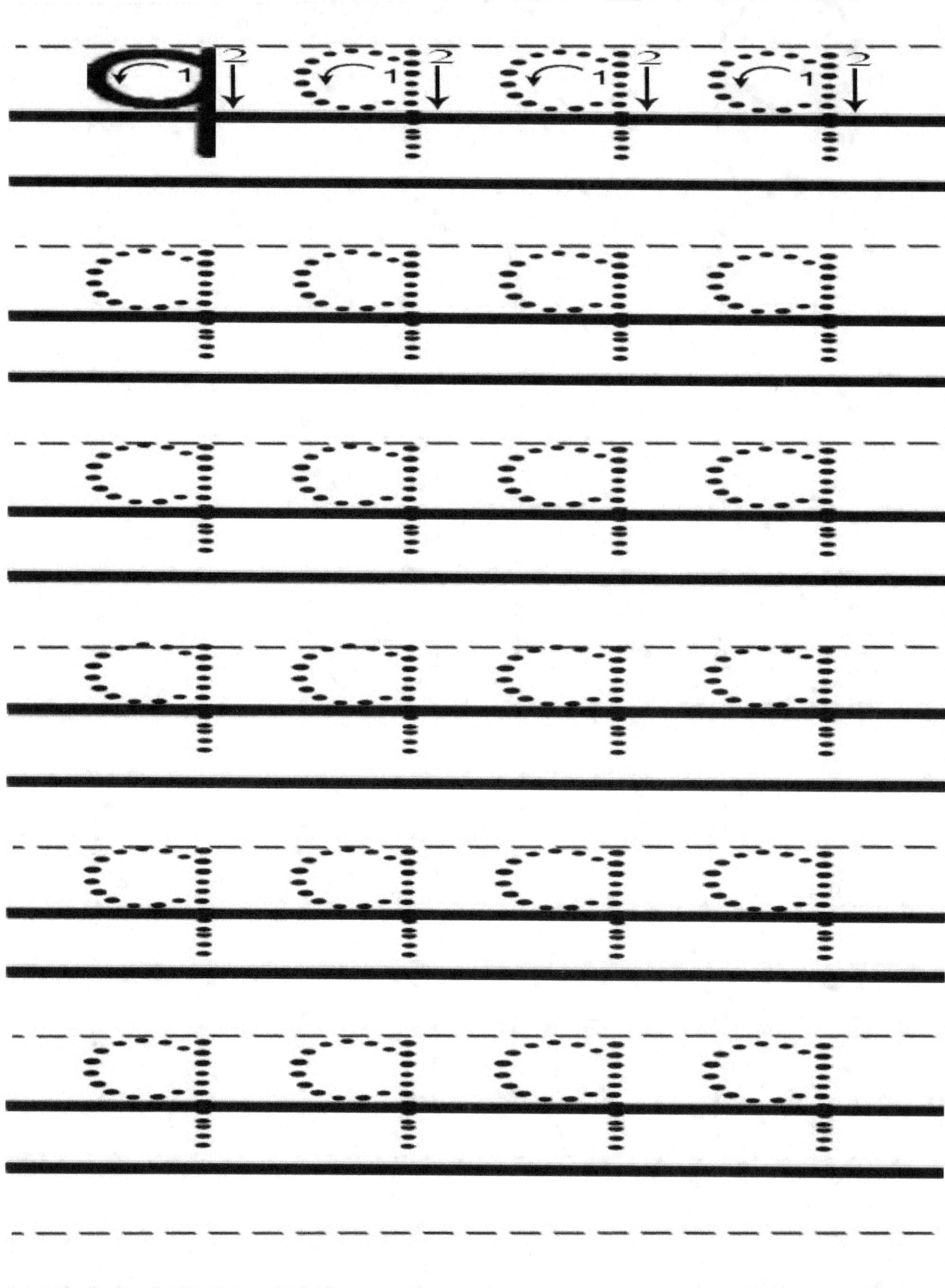

R is for

RABBIT

The Letter R

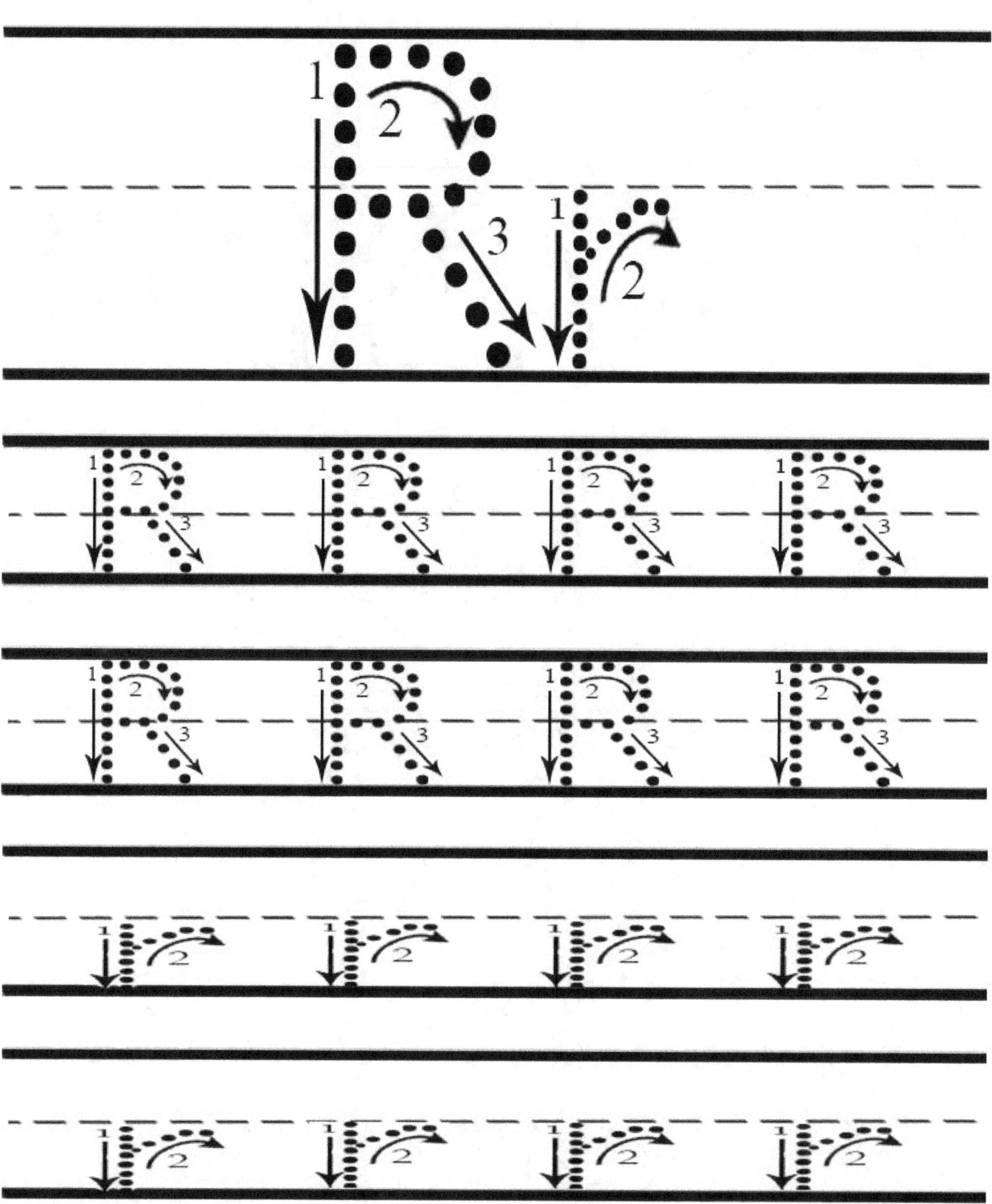

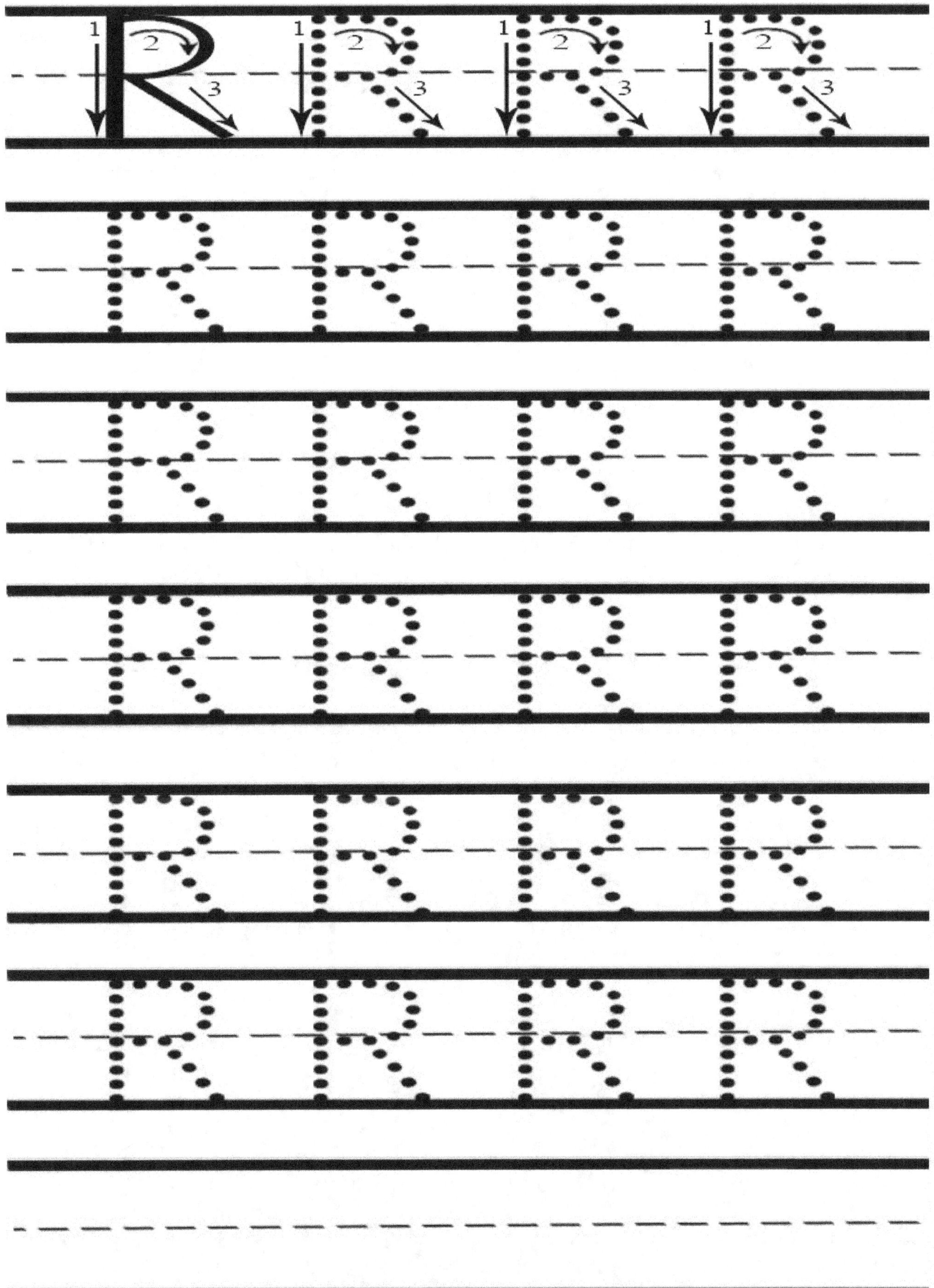

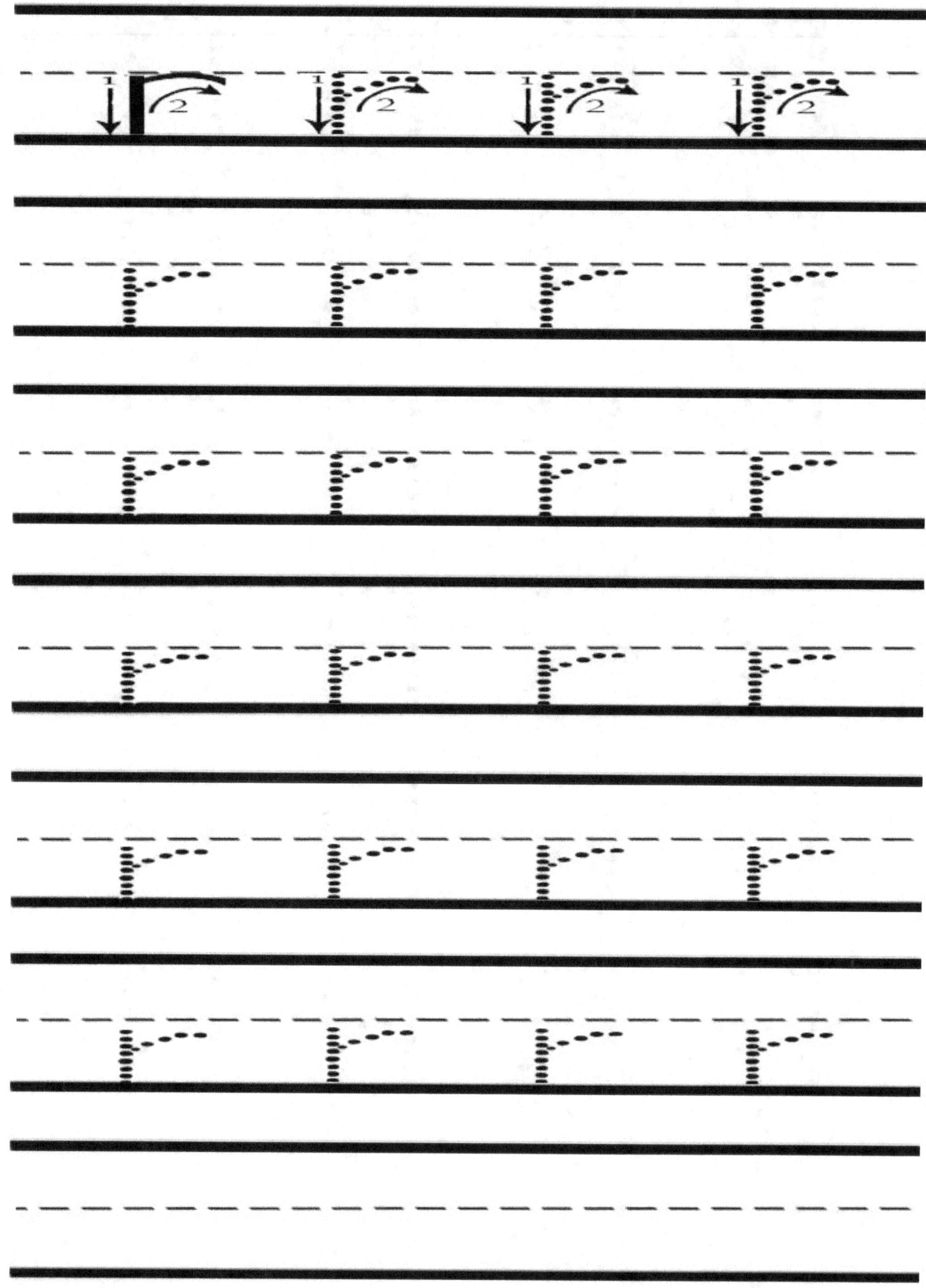

S is for

The Letter S

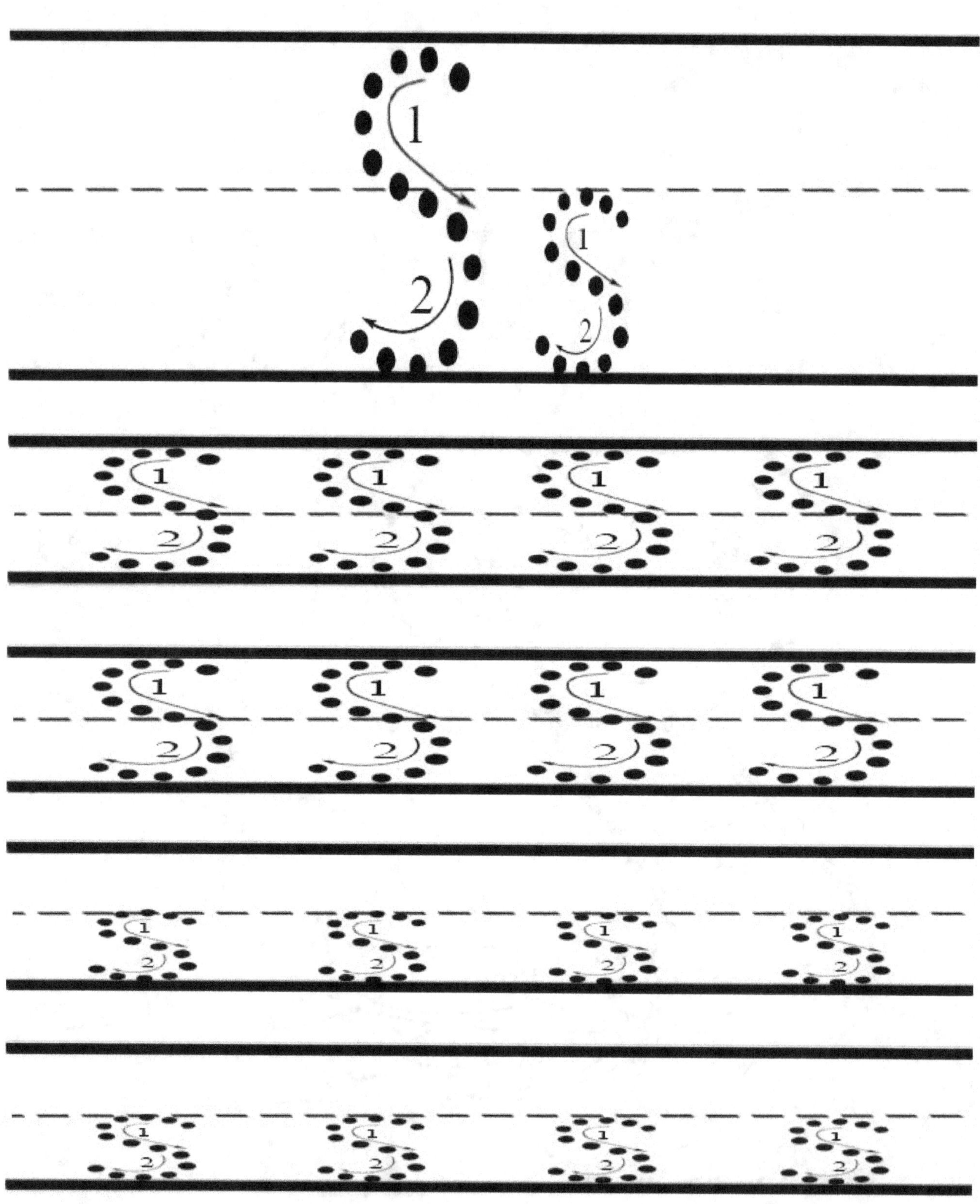

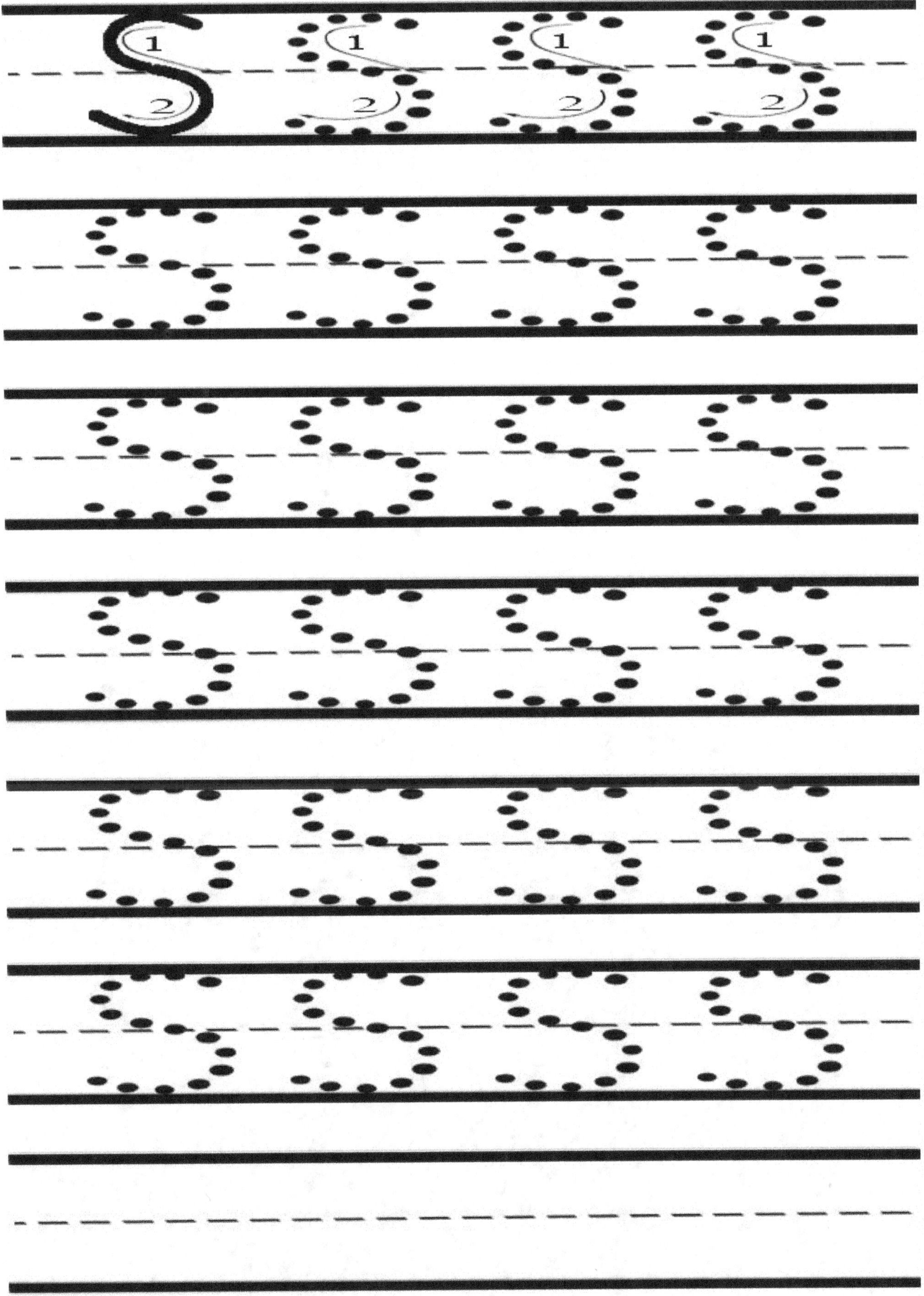

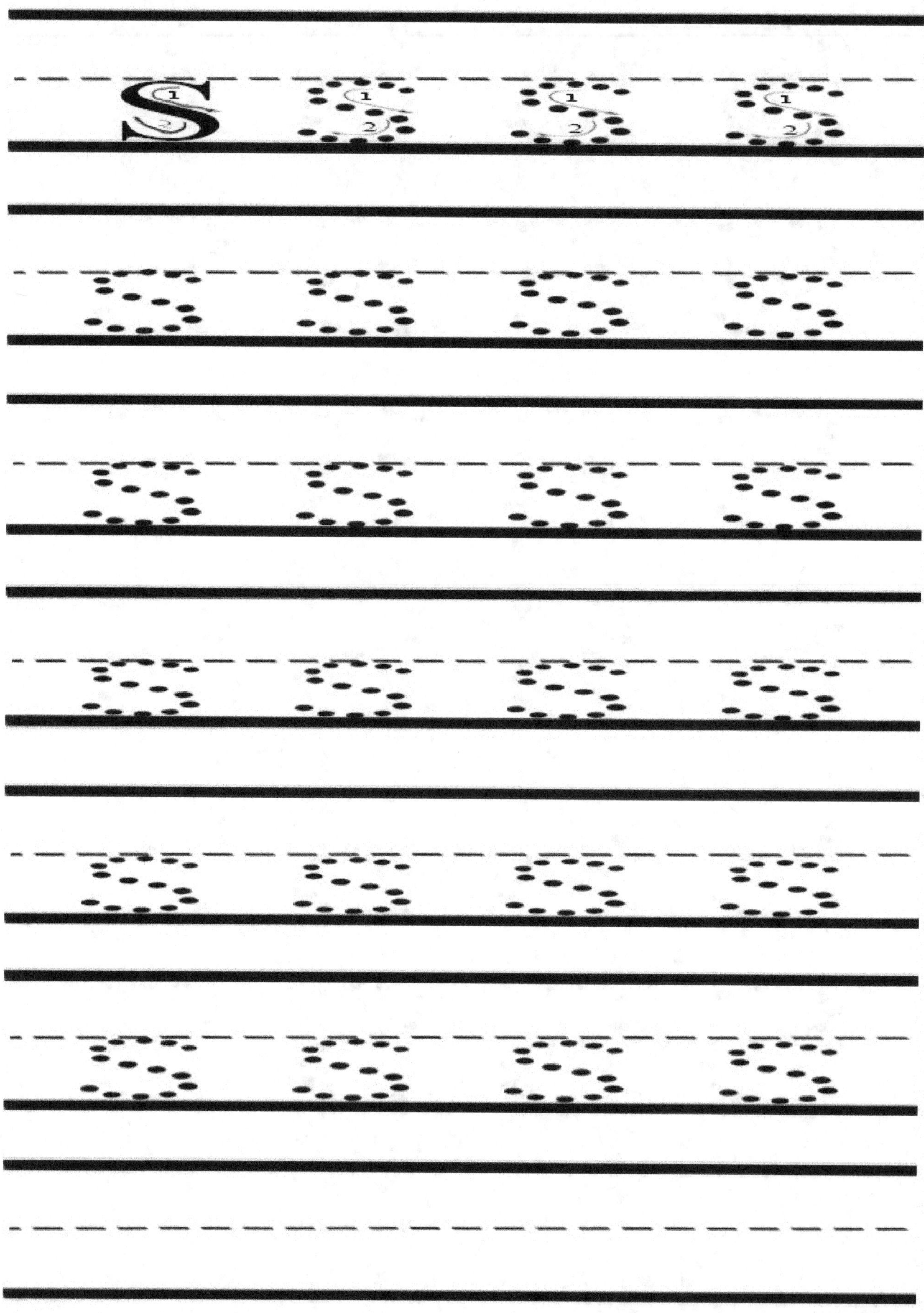

T is for

The Letter T

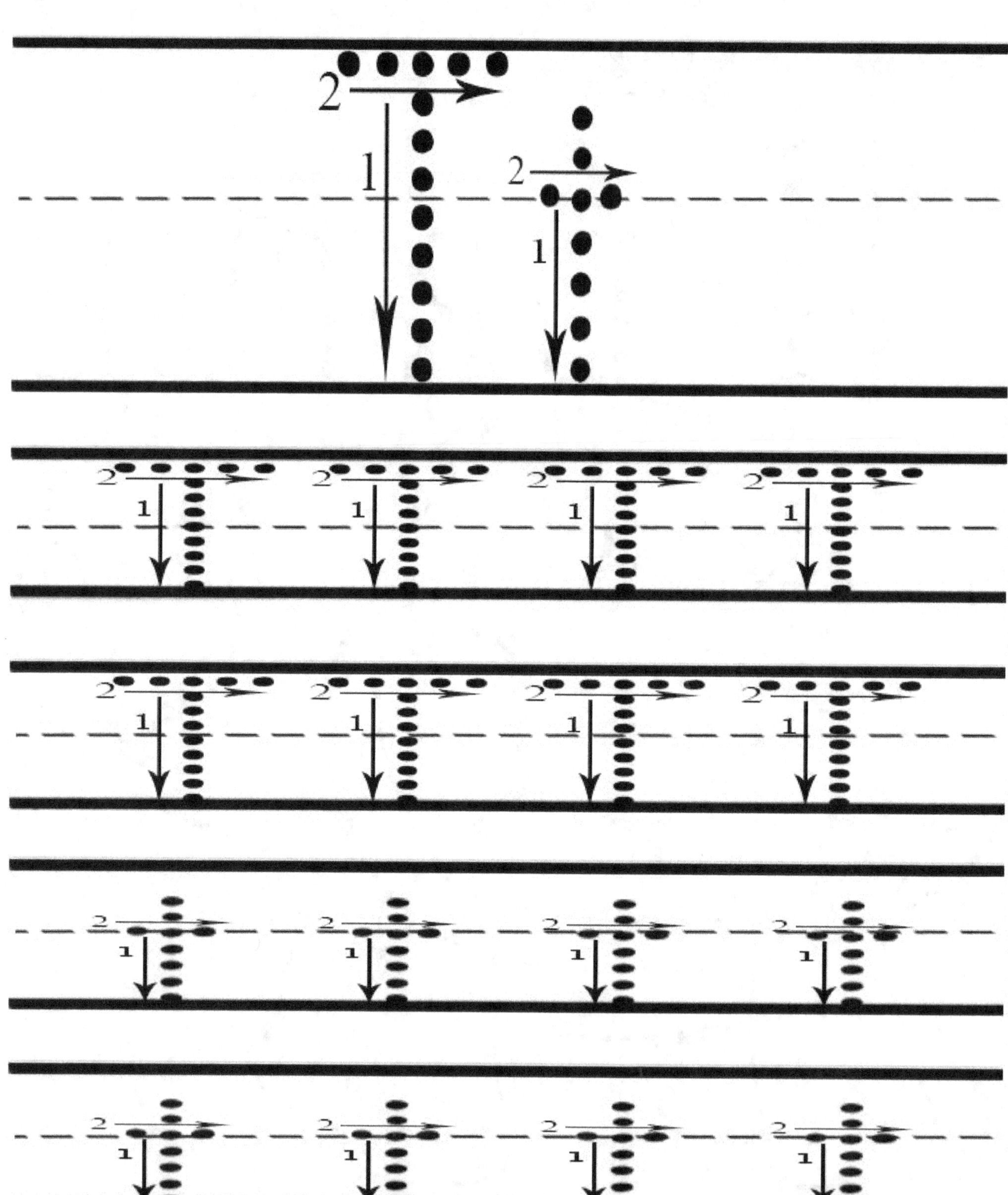

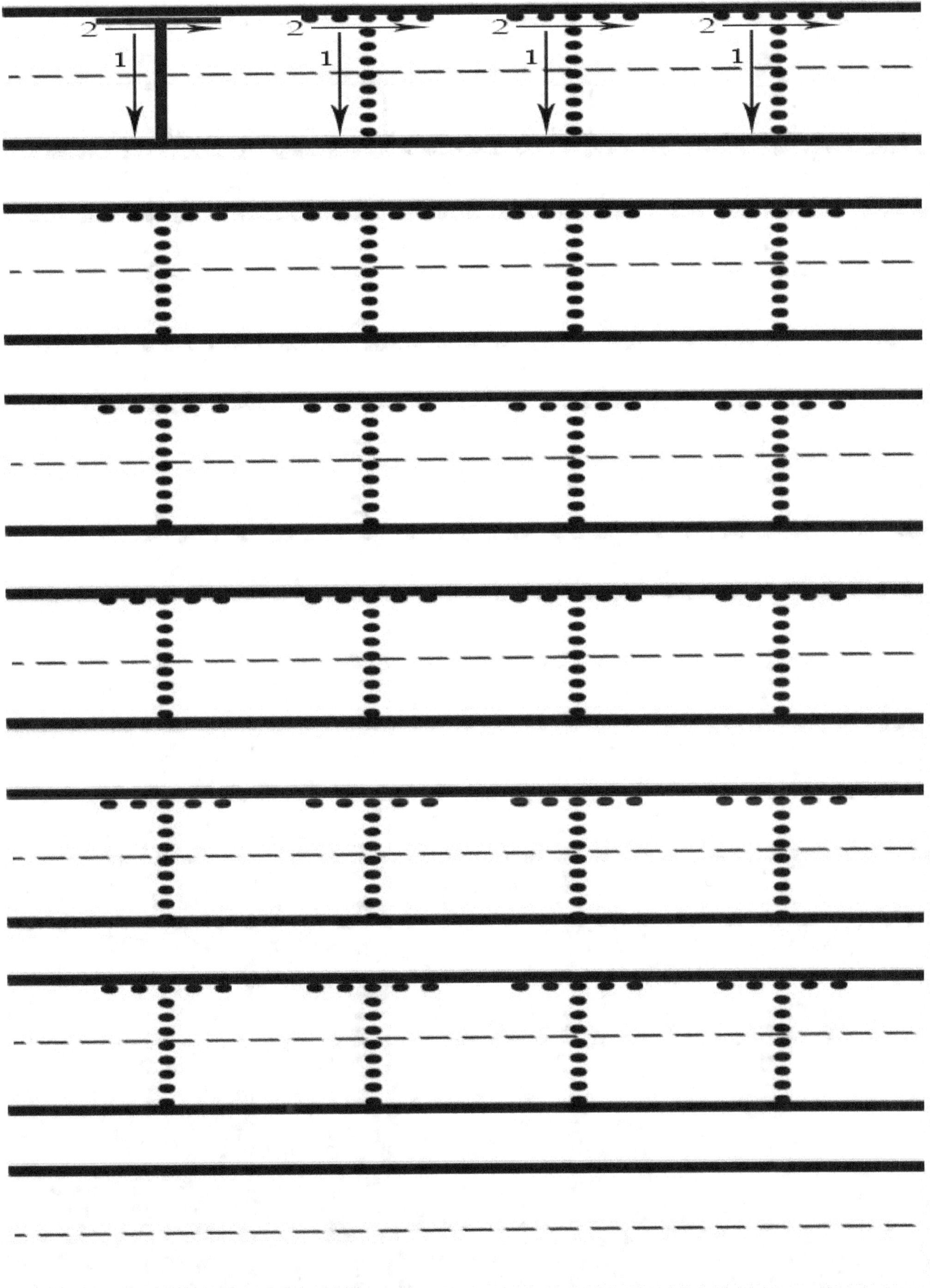

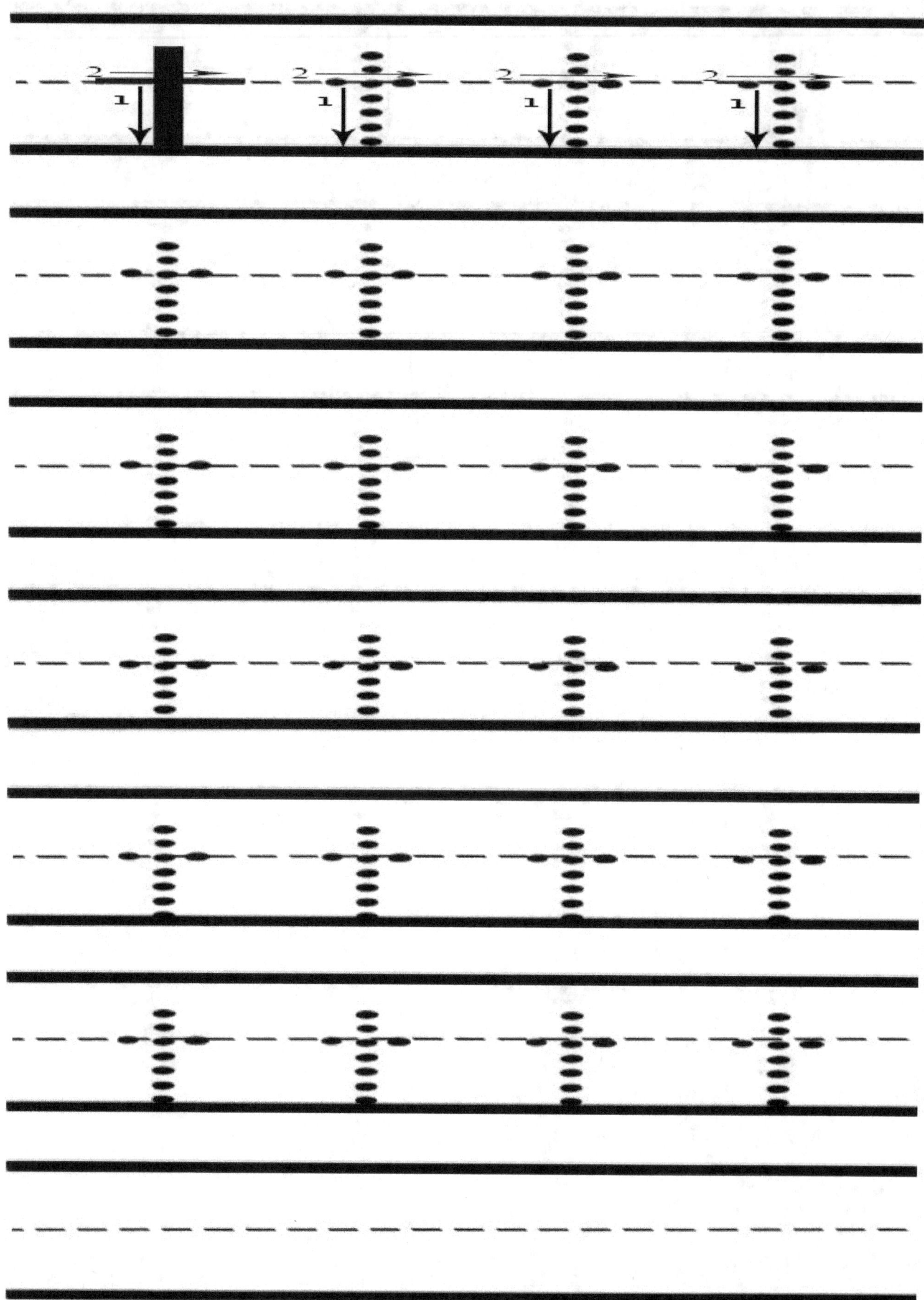

U is for

The Letter U

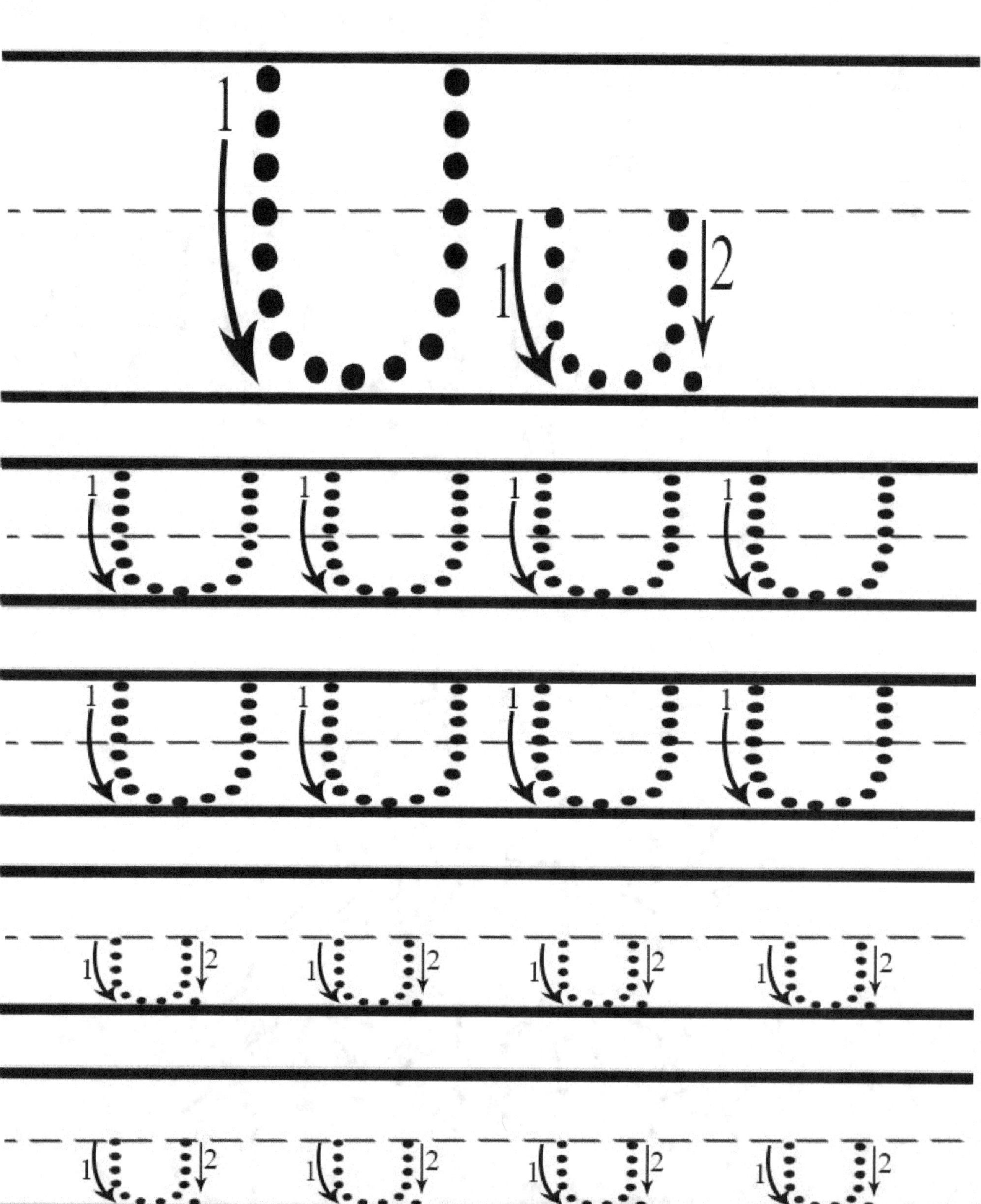

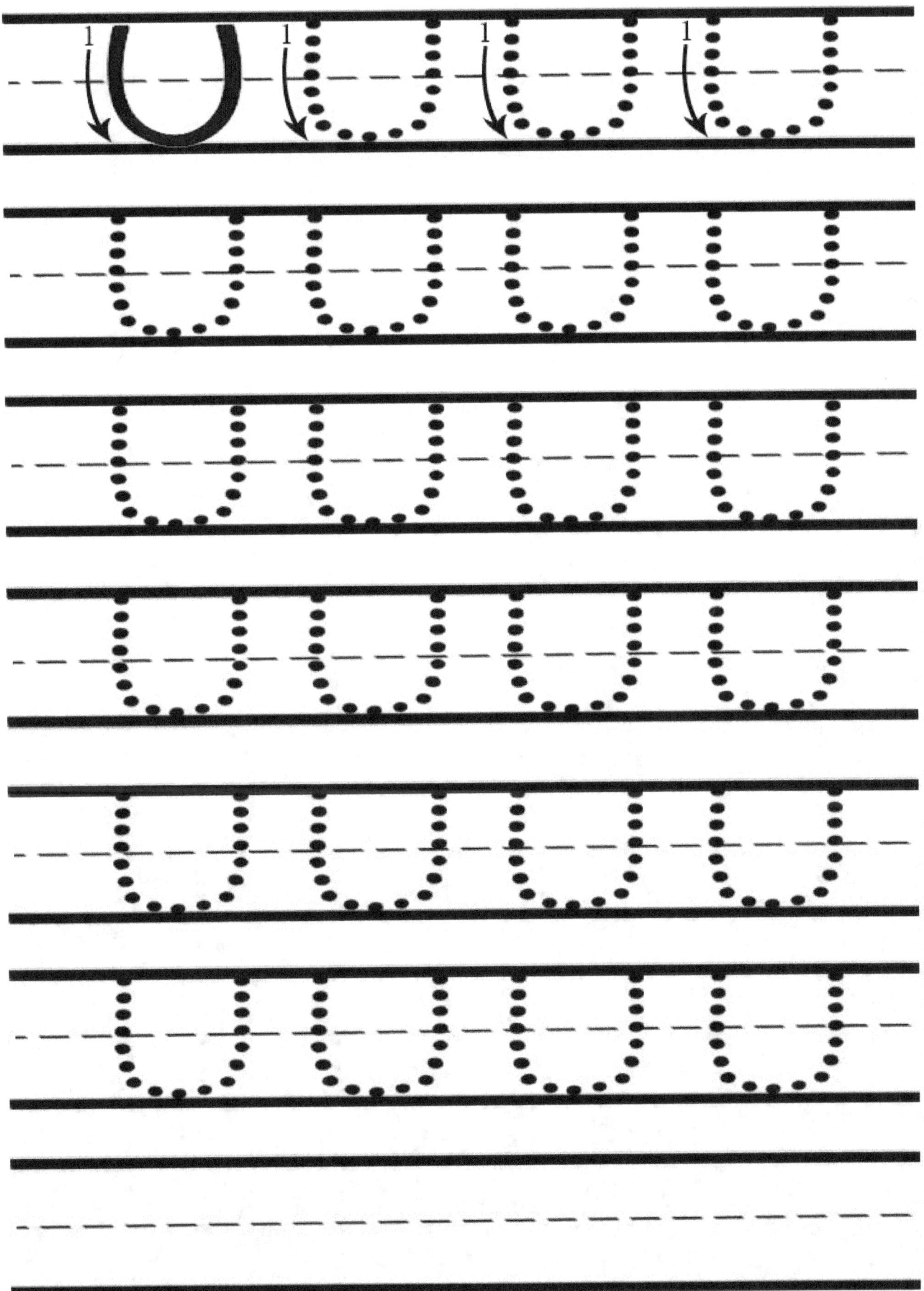

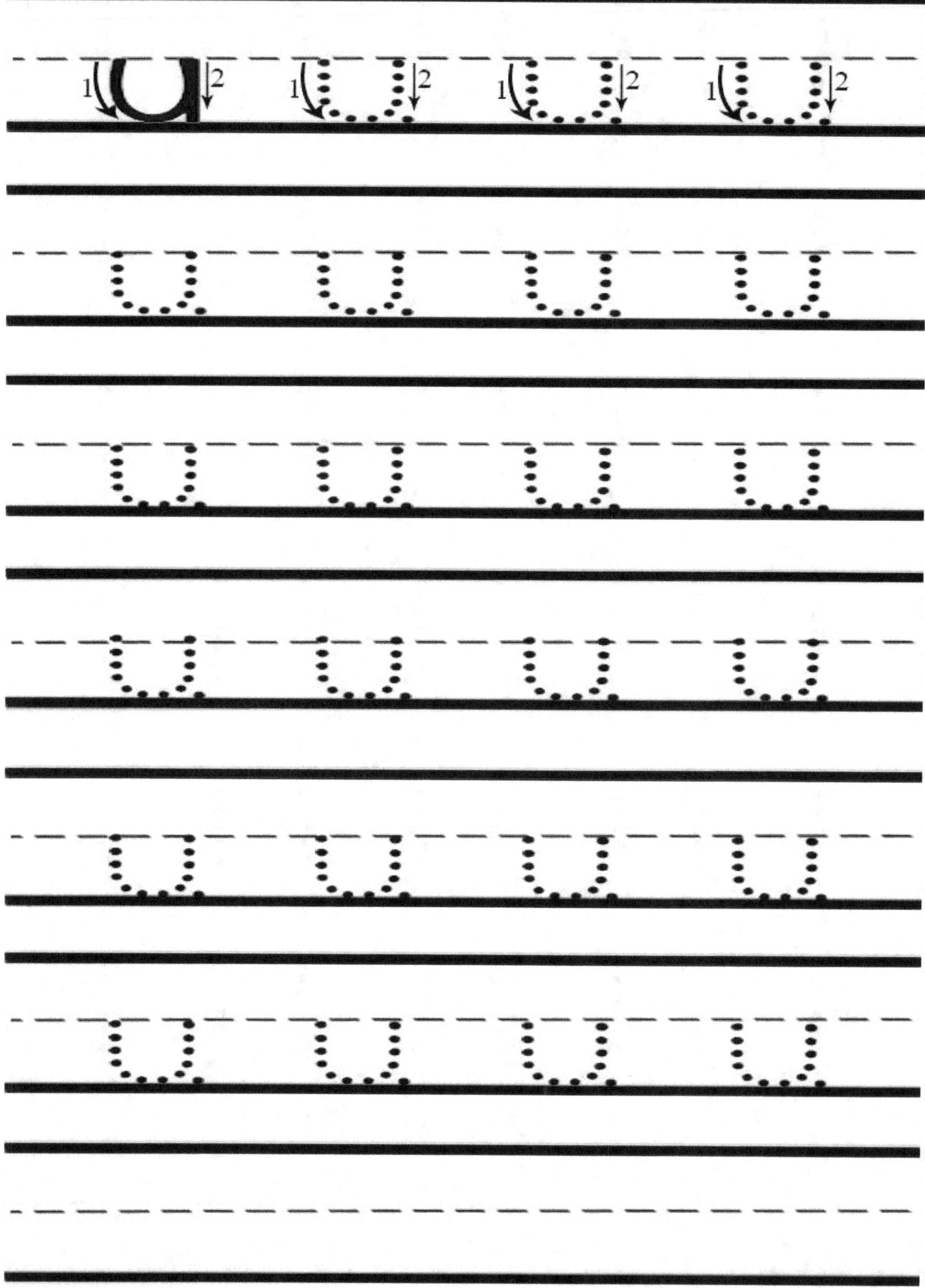

V is for

The Letter V

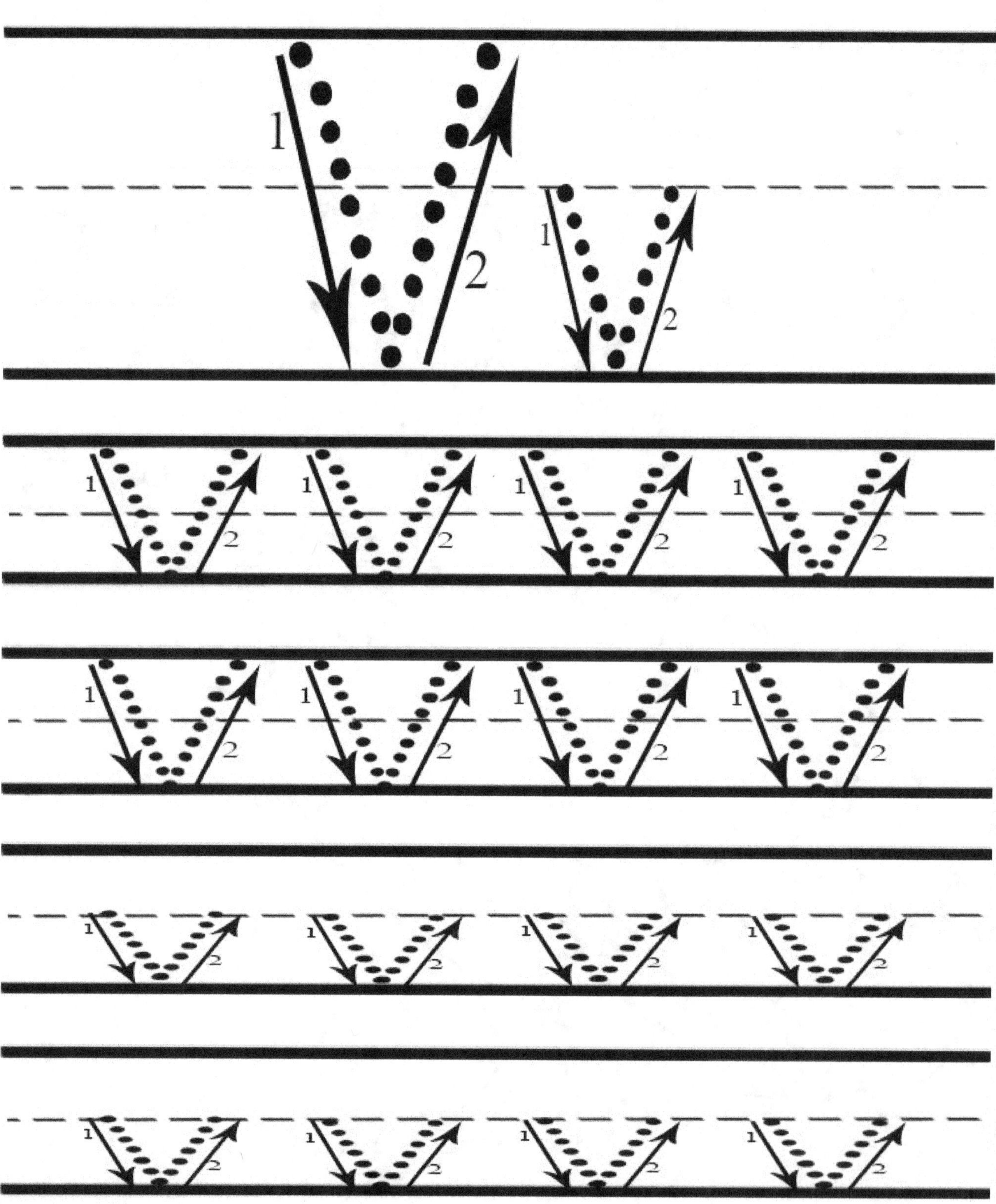

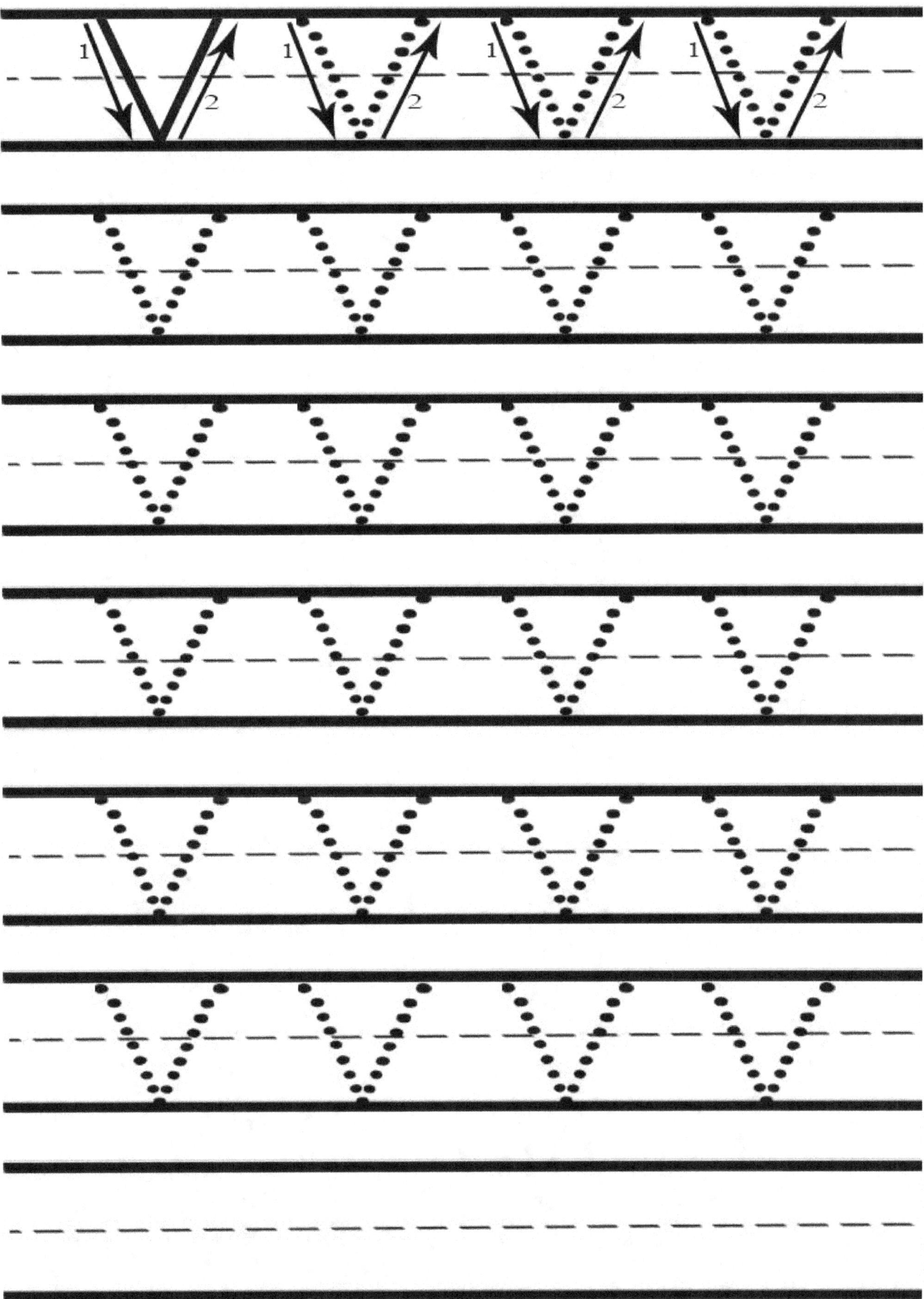

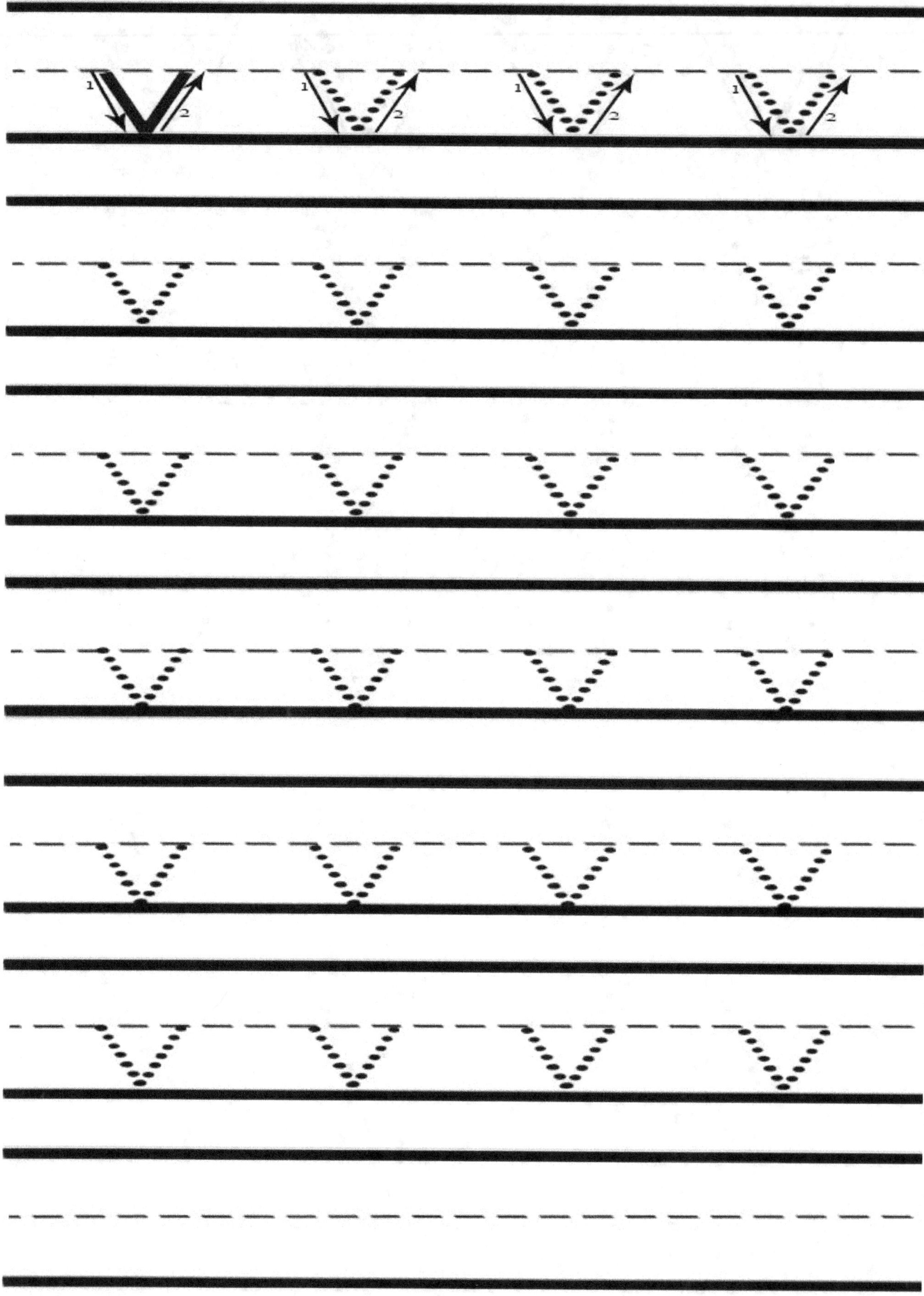

W is for

The Letter W

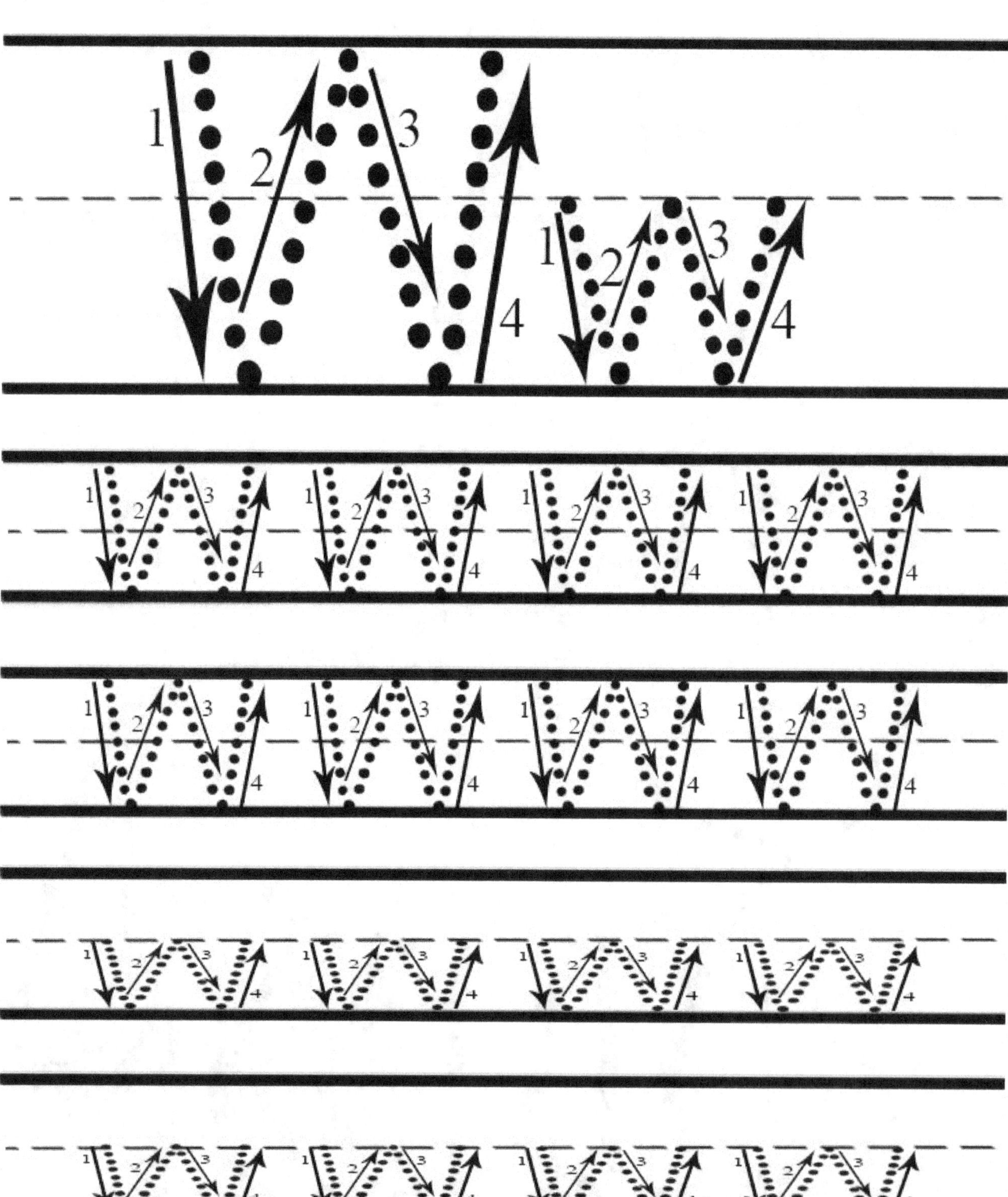

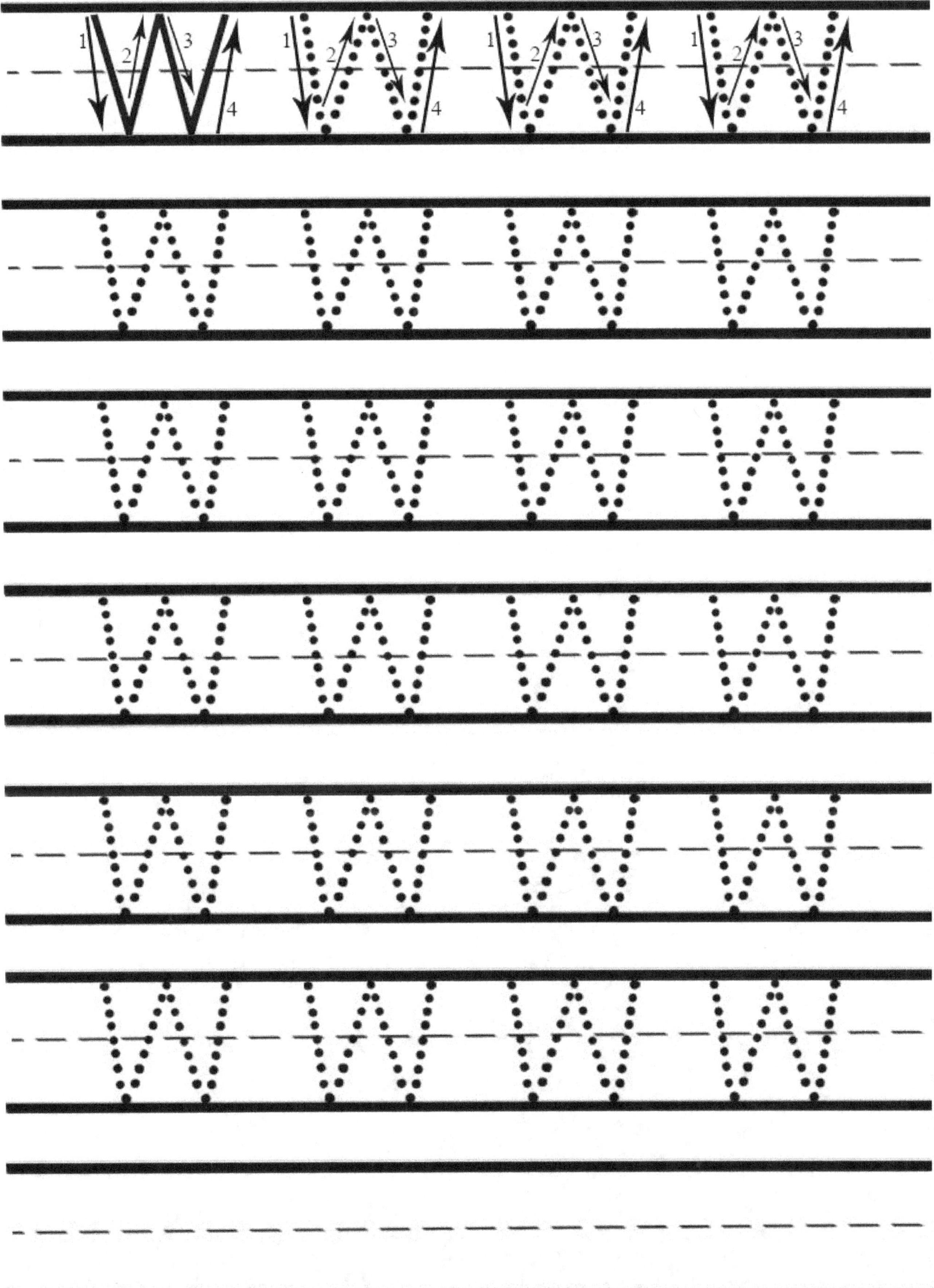

1 2 3 4   1 2 3 4   1 2 3 4   1 2 3 4

X is for

The Letter X

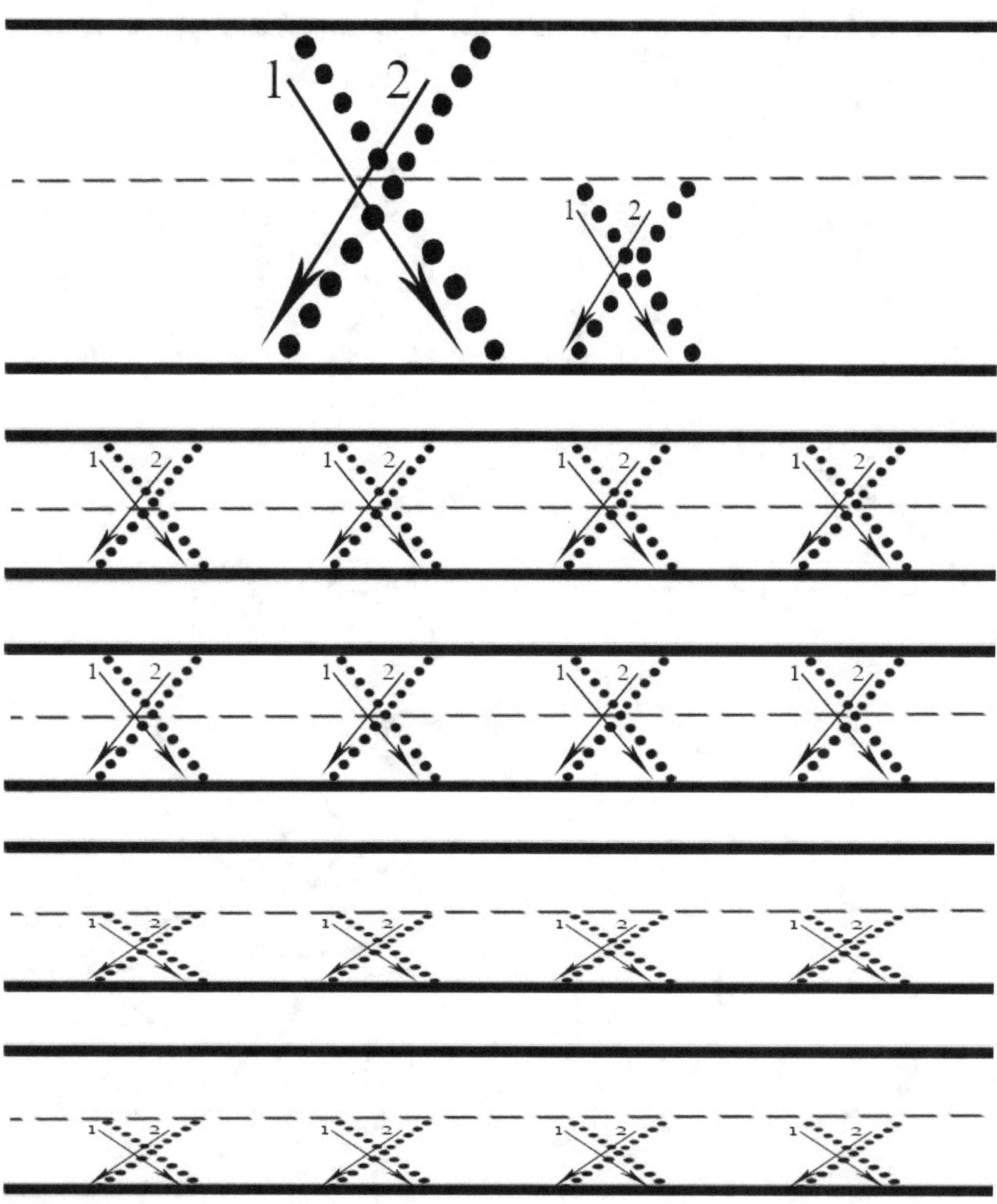

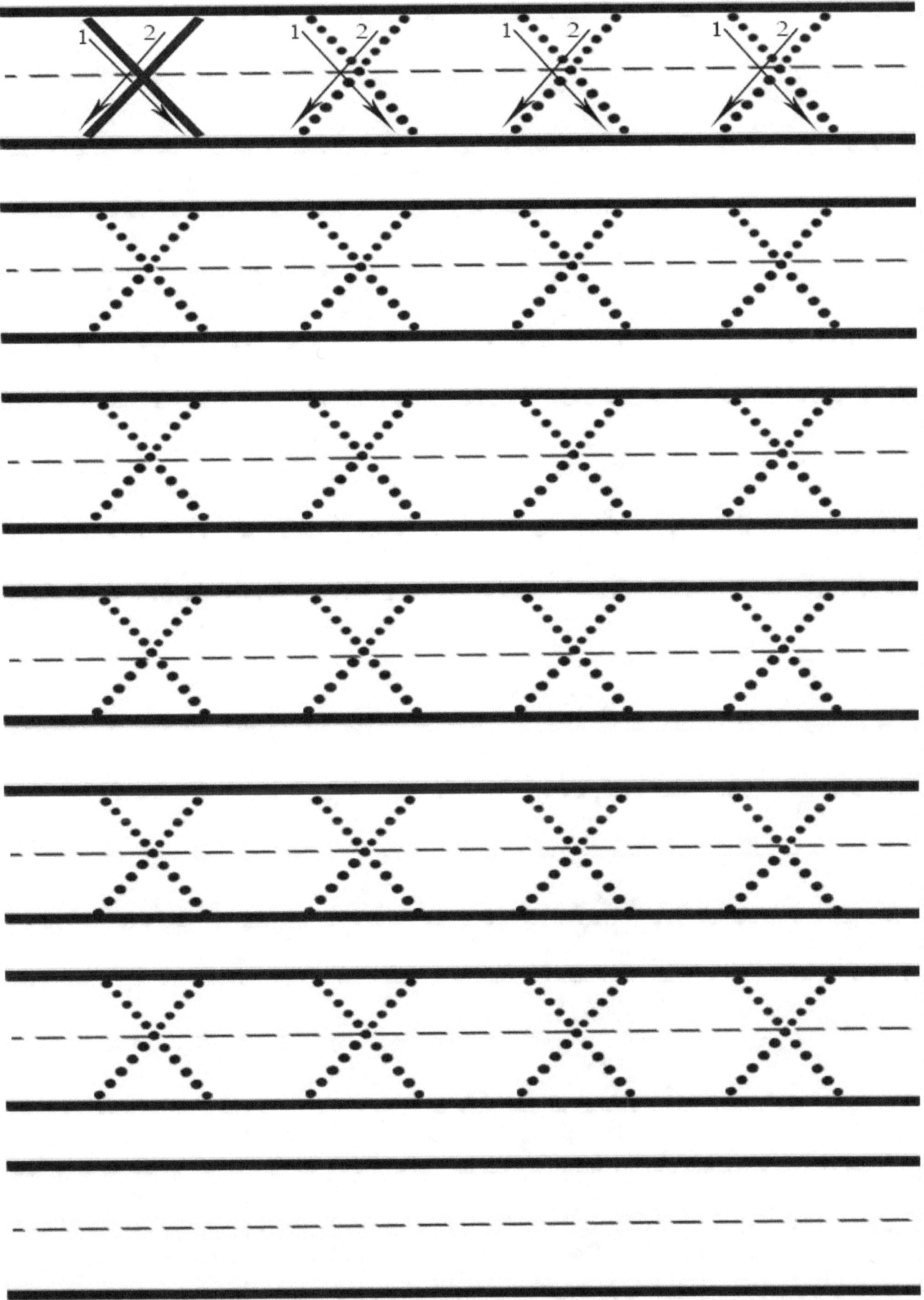

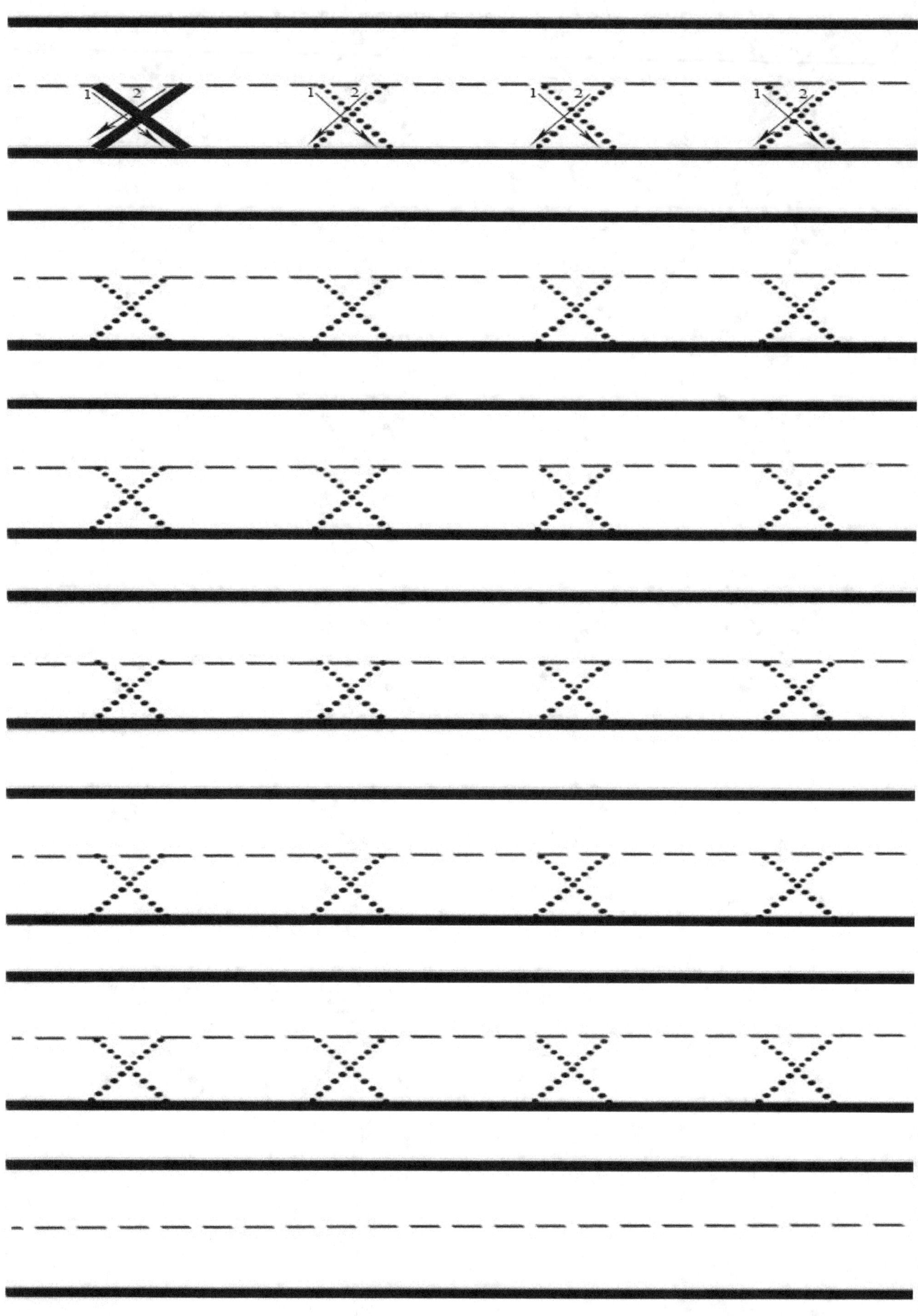

Y is for

The Letter Y

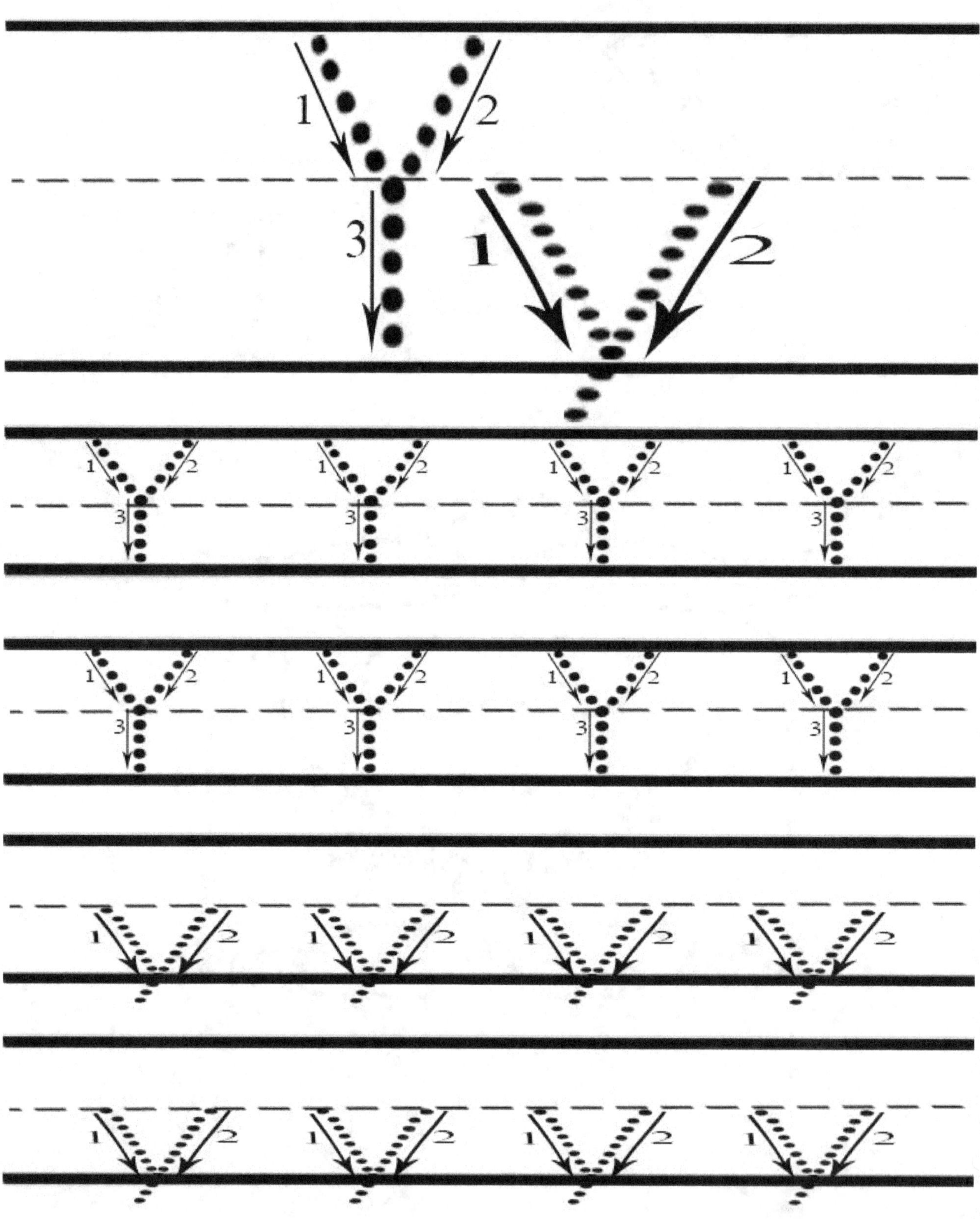

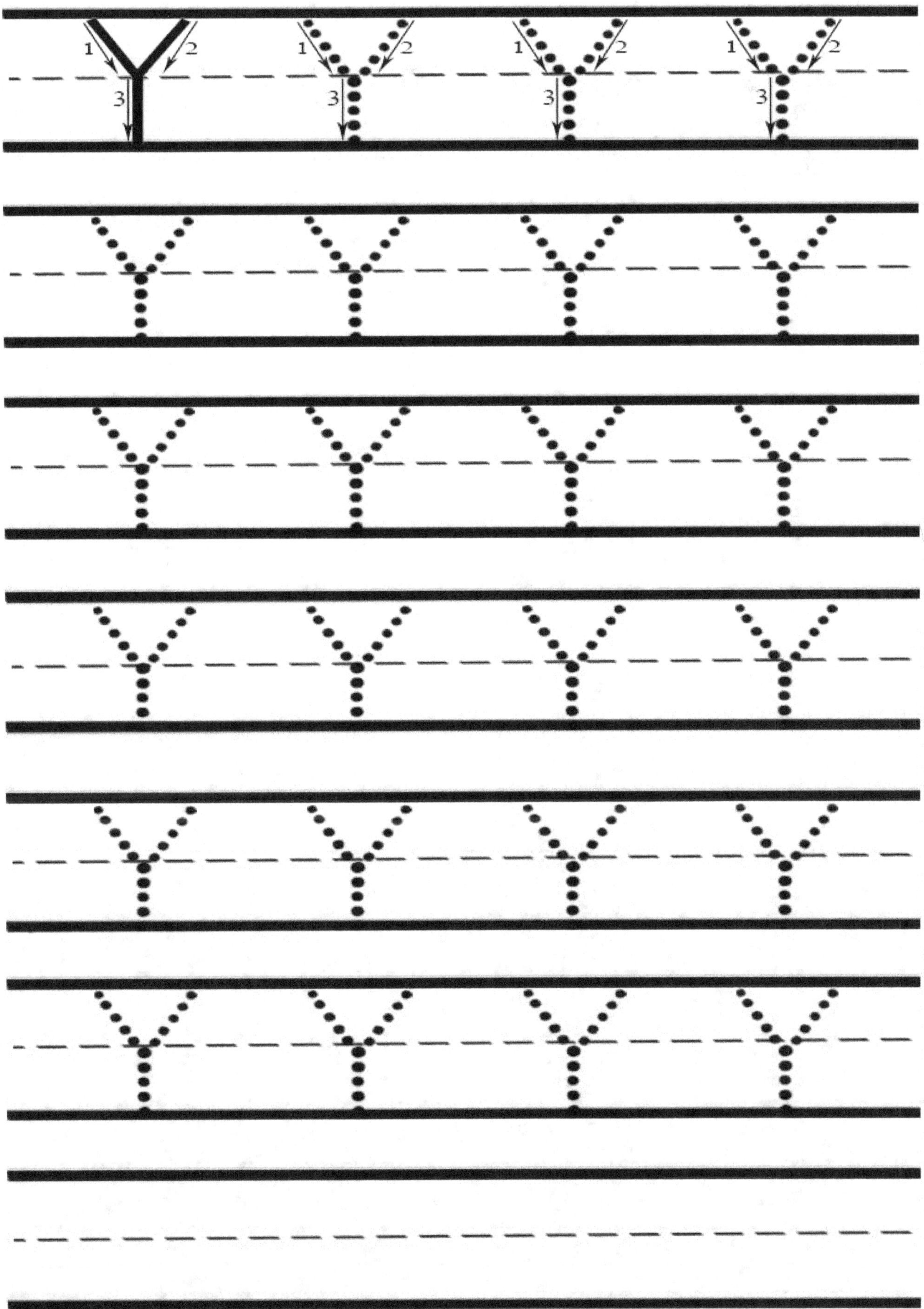

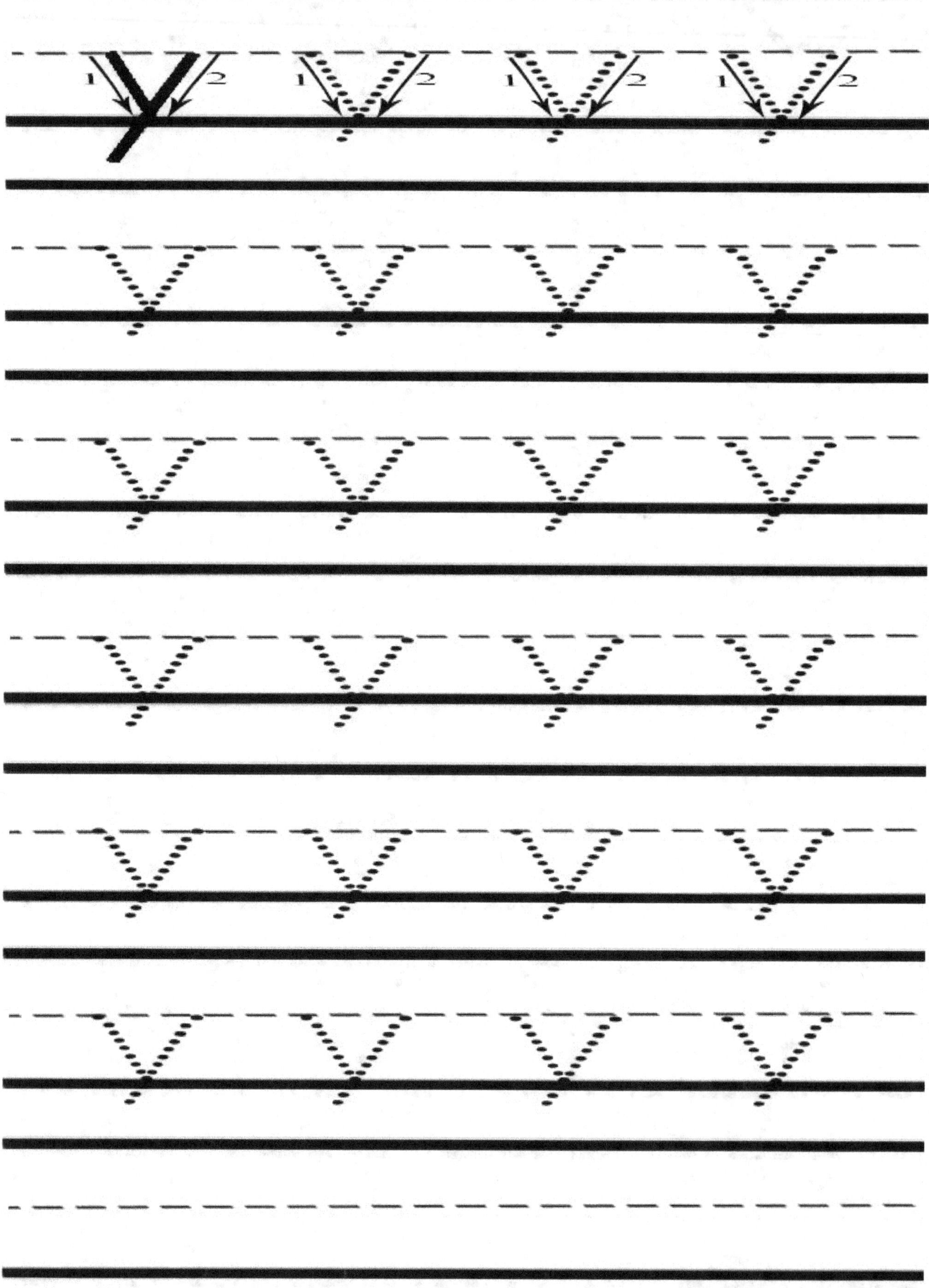

Z is for

The Letter Z

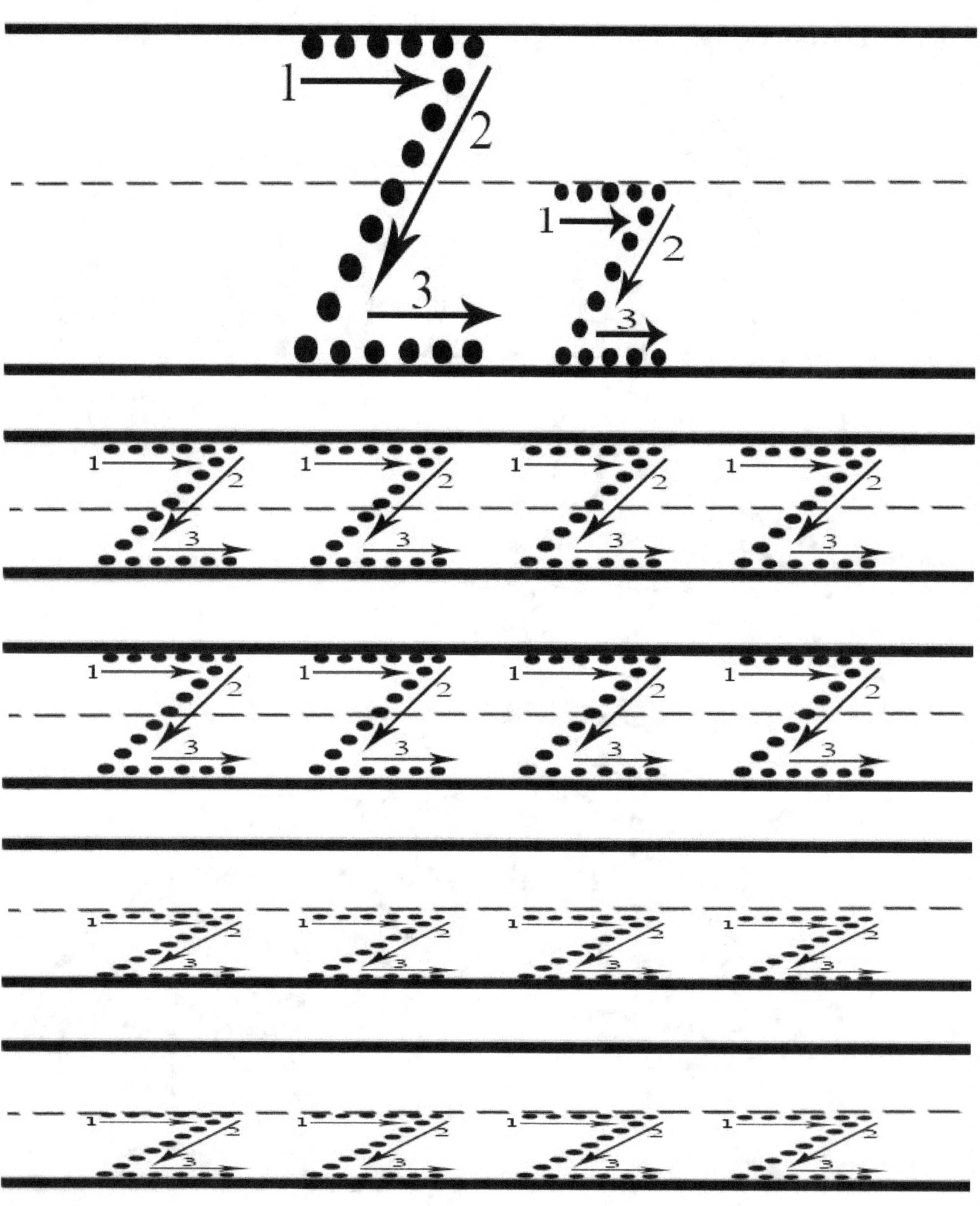

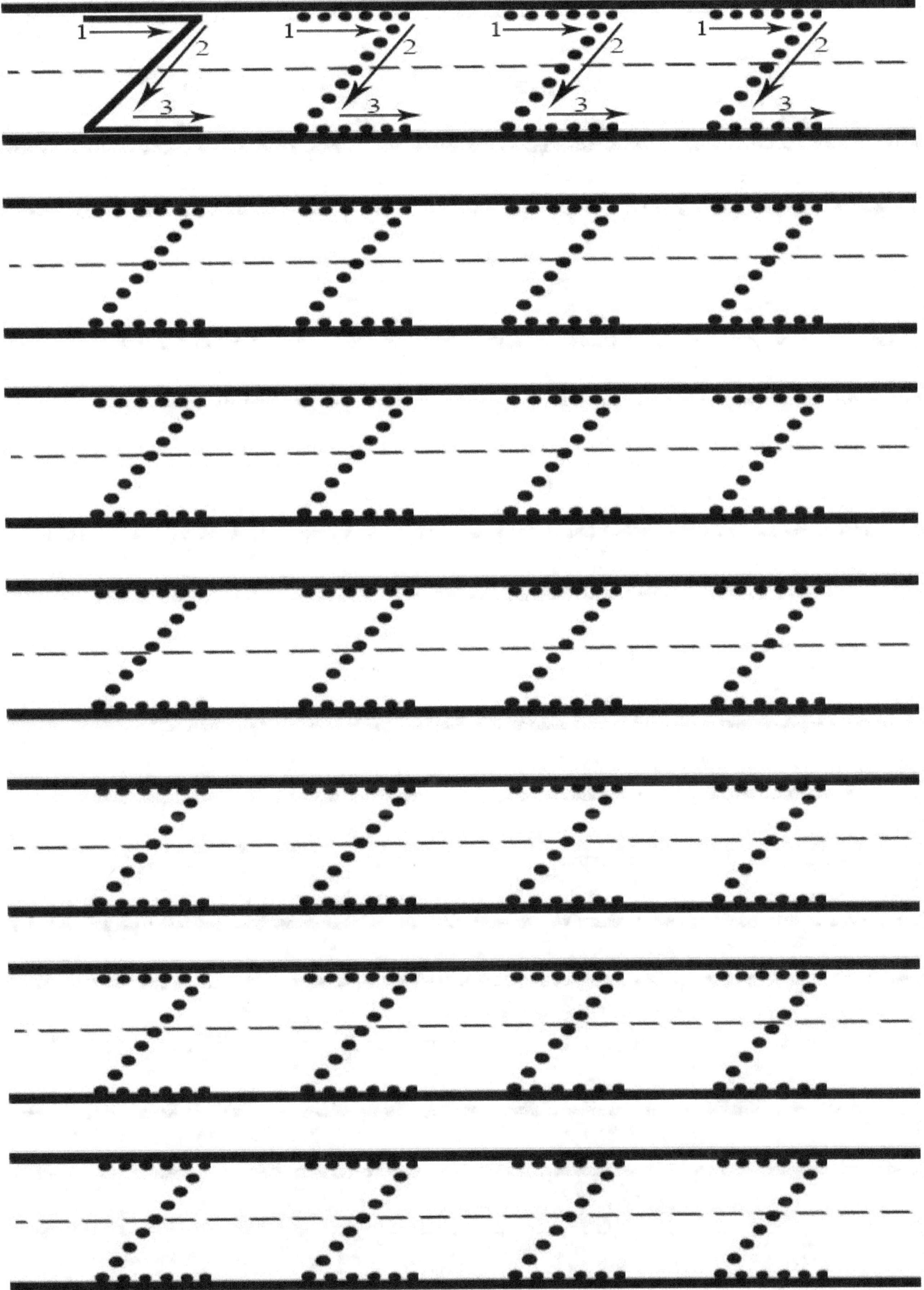

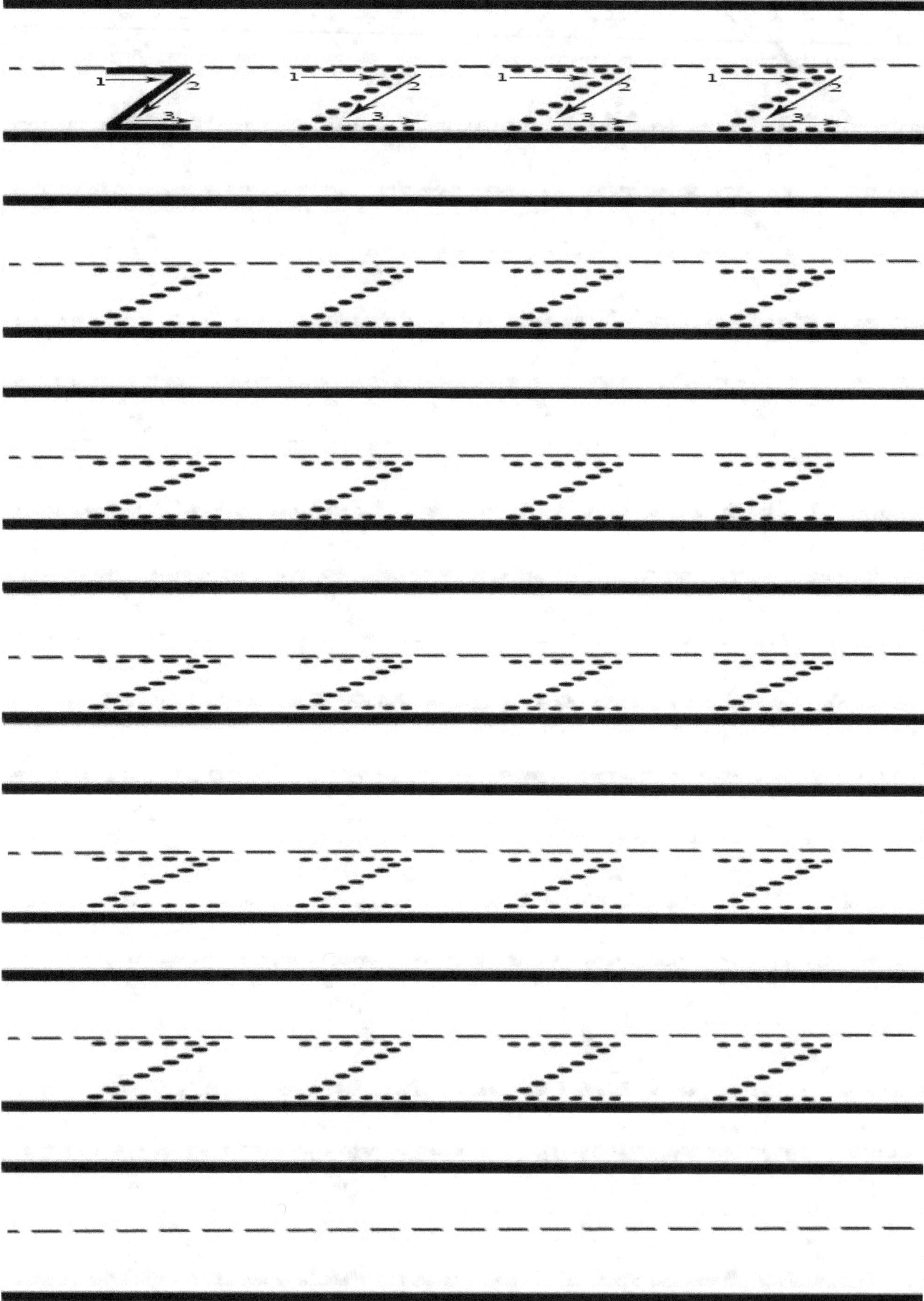

I CAN write my